NOW IS THE BEST TIME EVER TO OWE THE IRS

Richard M. Schickel

Now is the Best Time Ever to Owe the IRS

Copyright 2021© R.M.S. Tax Consulting LLC

All rights reserved. No part of this book may be used or reproduced in any manner whatsoever without written permission of the author except in the case of brief quotations embodied in critical articles or reviews.

Interior Formatting by Melissa Williams Design

Edited by Katherine Thompson of Paris & Cosmo LLC, Tucson, AZ

DEDICATION

I dedicate this book to the American taxpayer. The many men and woman who go to work and pay their taxes because they want to do the right thing. They want to pay their "fair share" of the tax burden because it is the right thing to do.

They learned in kindergarten that we should share, play fair and not take things that don't belong to them.

This book is dedicated to all the people in the tax industry, the Enrolled Agents, Accountants, Lawyers and employees who make the tax system actually work.

I dedicate this book to the Internal Revenue Service employees past and present who struggle to serve the American people despite the burden of poor tax administration.

NOTICE FROM AUTHOR AND PUBLISHER

The author and publisher disclaim all liability for any damages resulting from the application presented in this book. All names, dates, and case circumstances are compilations and have been sanitized to prevent disclosure of confidential tax information. This book is designed to share the authors findings and opinions based on life experiences, research, analysis and experience with the subject matter covered. This information is not provided for purposes of rendering tax, legal, accounting or other professional advice. If tax, legal or accounting advice is required, the services of a qualified attorney, CPA or Enrolled Agent should be sought.

NOW IS THE BEST TIME EVER TO OWE THE IRS

> It's not how much money you make,
> But how much money you keep,
> How hard it works for you,
> And how many generations you keep it.
>
> **Robert T. Kiyosaki**

This book has been especially written as a self-help guide for those taxpayers who owe the IRS back taxes and for those taxpayers who may owe the IRS taxes once the pandemic is over. The IRS has antiquated computers and is grossly understaffed. Historically, the IRS has been rather secretive, sharing taxpayer's rights with them. This book reveals secrets that the IRS does not want you to know. By understanding how the IRS works, paying past-due taxes has never been easier.

The United States IRS Tax Code, as it is currently written, provides a system where Rich People, Big Businesses, and Corporations have massive tax breaks compared to the average taxpayer. The IRS tax code was made even more inequitable by President Trump's Tax Cuts and Jobs Act in 2017.

In order to change the system, taxpayers need to realize what changes need to be made in order to have a reasonable and fair tax code. This easy-to-read book will help you understand why some politicians try to divert our attention to other issues to keep taxpayers from realizing that the majority of us are supporting the very wealthy. Knowledge is power. Voters need to know how best to protect their money and not get side-tracked by emotional and political issues we cannot control. Reading this easily to understandable book about taxes will arm you with that information to make your vote count.

Table of Contents

Introduction	xii
Chapter 1: What Happened?	1
Chapter 2: How Did You Get in Trouble with the IRS?	12
Chapter 3: Post-Traumatic I.R.S Disorder—the Pandemic's Effect on the IRS and the Chaos that Awaits	23
Chapter 4: How Differently Does the I.R.S Treat Rich People, Big Businesses, Corporations, and You?	32
Chapter 5: How to Fight the IRS—Knowledge is Power	41
Exhibit #1: *Notice of Federal Tax Lien*	47
Exhibit #2: *IRS Transcript Type*	48
Exhibit #3: *Get Your Tax Record*	50
Exhibit #4: *Exhibit Sign Up*	52
Exhibit #5: *You Will Need to Register*	53
Exhibit #6: *You Will Need Some Information About Yourself to Register*	54
Exhibit #7: *You Will Need a Financial Account to Register*	55
Exhibit #8: *You Need a Phone Number or Verified Address*	56
Exhibit #9: *Let's Get Started!*	57
Exhibit #10: *View Your Account Information*	58
Chapter 6: Do I Need a Tax Professional to Get the Best Deal?	60
Chapter 7: Audits Are for Everyone, Even Criminals	69
Chapter 8: IRS Secrets Revealed	80
Chapter 9: How to Respond to the IRS	94
Chapter 10: How to Get the Best Installment Agreement from the IRS	103
Chapter 11: Currently Not Collectible—When You Cannot Pay Your Back Taxes Now or Ever	119
Chapter 12: IRS Penalties and Interest	127
Chapter 13: When Do You Need to Prepare Form 433–A/B Financial Statements?	143
Exhibit #11: *Collection National Standards*	159

Exhibit #12: *2021 Allowable Living Expenses Health Care Standards*	159
Exhibit #13: *Local Standards Housing and Utilities*	160
Exhibit #14: *Allowable Living Expenses Transportation Standards*	164
Chapter 14: Why Is Your Case Assigned to a Revenue Officer?	166
Chapter 15: What Kind of Deals Can You Make with the IRS Collection?	174
Chapter 16: IRS Targets for the Years 2021–2022	186
Chapter 17: How Do the *Rich People* Get Away with Not Paying Taxes?	191
Chapter 18: A Professional View for the Solution to the Tax Gap	198
Epilogue	201
IRS Abbreviations	213
Acknowledgments	215
Also by Richard M. Schickel	216
About the Author	217
Sources	219

These Supplements can be found online at TaxReliefforYou.com and are not included in the paper edition of the book:

Supplement A
How Much Do You Pay in Taxes

Supplement B
How to Prepare a Collection Financial Statement

Supplement C
What You Need to Know About Your Chances for an Audit

Supplement D
The Truth About Offers in Compromise

Supplement E
What Kind of Deals Can You Make with IRS Collection

Supplement F
Appeals + Tax Court

Supplement G
List of Installment Agreements

Supplement H
Map of Where Revenue Officer Case Work is Located

INTRODUCTION

Taxes are what you pay for a civilized society.

—Justice Oliver Wendall Homes

I have to apologize. This is a book about the IRS and taxes. I know that reading about taxes and thinking about money can quickly exhaust anyone.

But stay with me.

This boring tax talk is how the rich and corporations get so filthy rich, and your standard of living and income declines year after year.

CHAPTER 1
WHAT HAPPENED?

When I grew up, a sole breadwinner would work, and the wife would stay home and had 3-6 kids. The father worked 40 hours a week and retired at age 60 with a pension and Social Security. He most likely owned the house they lived in, had a savings account, and owned a few stocks. Today, it takes two people working 40 hours a week, barely paying the rent and utilities. Survival is the main focus for Americans.

Additionally, the dollars that you are left with after taxes are just not worth as much either. Did you know that since 1980 the inflation rate is 240%? This means that what you could buy for $100 now will cost you $340.

All 535 members of Congress are responsible for the Tax Code, not the IRS Going back 70 years, members of Congress are personally responsible for the tax code's inequities. Many of these members have inserted thousands of special provisions to the tax code that benefit small groups of taxpayers who have lobbied Congress for special tax treatment.

President Trump signed the Tax Cuts and Jobs Act in 2017, and it is the signature legislative achievement of his administration. The law took away the ability to itemize deductions for most people. It hurt charities and the real estate market by limiting state and local property tax deductibility.

"The unfairness of the tax laws is unbelievable," Trump said in

2016. "It's been something I've been talking about for a long time, despite frankly being a big beneficiary of the laws. But now, I'm working for the American taxpayer. I'm not working for Trump anymore." —*Donald J. Trump*

Mr. Trump was correct. As a real estate developer, he received many benefits from the tax laws. Tax laws were all bought and paid for by lobbyists who made big bucks to wine and dine members of Congress. Thus, lobbyists would be able to influence tax bills that benefited their clients.

The Tax Cuts and Jobs Act in 2017 benefited very *Rich People, Big Businesses, and Corporations* exponentially. It expanded and enhanced several lucrative tax breaks for real estate developers. The law barred people and companies from avoiding capital gains taxes by selling one property and buying another, but the real estate industry was exempted. The real estate industry has enjoyed the most lucrative tax breaks for decades. The law allows real estate investors to depreciate property and sell the property and avoid any gain as long as they quickly purchase other properties. They are always postponing their gains well into the future. (Internal Revenue Code 1031 Exchange)

Historical preservation restricted easements also receive significant tax cuts that further increase the value of their properties but turn into significant deductions for the investor.

An apartment building or commercial building can be purchased for $270,000; then, the tax law allows the buyer to depreciate (deduct) the value by $10,000 a year for the next 27 years ($270,000). If a building is kept in a good state of repair and not allowed to turn into a slum property, it will almost always be worth more when it is eventually sold.

Mr. Trump will personally get $15 million more due to the very tax cuts he signed. Trillions of dollars will be transferred from the working poor and middle class to rich people and corporations in the next thirty years because of these new tax laws.

Many rich people like to advertise that they pay taxes. However, most pay taxes on only a small portion of their income. Millionaires and billionaires don't suffer as you do when you pay your taxes out of the measly amount paid for working your life away for some corporation. *Rich People* do not pay their fair share of taxes, this needs to stop!

A recent series of stories by ProPublica (https://www.propublica.org/article/the-secret-IRS-files-trove-of-never-before-seen-records-reveal-how-the-wealthiest-avoid-income-tax) used actual tax data to show that ProPublica has obtained a vast trove of Internal Revenue Service data on the tax returns of thousands of the nation's wealthiest people, covering more than 15 years. The data provides an unprecedented look inside the financial lives of America's titans, including Warren Buffett, Bill Gates, Rupert Murdoch, and Mark Zuckerberg. It shows not just their income and taxes but also their investments, stock trades, gambling winnings, and even the results of audits.

Here is the breakdown-Jeff Bezos (worth $196 billion) pays taxes at the .98% rate, Elon Musk (worth $165 billion) pays taxes at the 1.30% tax rate, Michael Bloomberg (worth $96 Billion) pays taxes at the 1.30% tax rate and Warren Buffett (worth $96 billion), per Propublica, pays taxes at the .10% tax rate.

Senator Bernie Sanders has called the accumulation of wealth by Jeff Bezos "Morally Obscene!" "He published this example: "Wealth of Jeff Bezos in 2009: $6.8 billion Wealth of Jeff Bezos in 2020: $184 billion Wealth of Mark Zuckerberg in 2009: $2 billion Wealth of Mark Zuckerberg in 2020: $103 billion US. Minimum Wage from 2009-2020: $7.25. We need an economy that works for all of us, not just the 1%."

Buffett, who broke ranks with his billionaire cohort to call for higher taxes on the rich, is an anomaly. The phrase "Do as I say, not as I do" fits him well. In a famous New York Times op-ed in 2011, Buffett wrote, "My friends and I have been coddled long enough by a billionaire-friendly Congress. It's time for our government to get serious about shared sacrifice."

Buffett and his fellow billionaires have known this secret for a long time. As Buffett put it in 2011: "There's been class warfare going on for the last 20 years, and my class has won."

A person earning $1 million a year will pay as much as 37% in taxes to IRS, which is $370,000, so they still have $630,000 left. (A lot of money!)

Now think about a worker who earns $100,000 a year and pays $28,000 (28%) in taxes; they would only have $73,000—not a lot of money for a family of four these days. Don't forget they need to pay Social Security taxes also. This further cuts into the money for living expenses.

Corporations, who have been cheating on their taxes for years, got the biggest rewards. Their tax rate dropped by 40% (from 39% down to 21%). Corporations are now allowed to shift income and profits to foreign countries to avoid taxes in the USA.

On top of that, rich people and business owners got a bonus tax cut in the 20% deduction for pass-through income. Pass-through income means that a person who owns a partnership, S corporation, or sole proprietorship would only be taxed on 80% of their income, not the full 100% profit that they made (as the poor or middle-class taxpayer would be taxed). Additionally, Trump's Tax Cuts and Jobs Act in 2017 added another deliberately confusing tax cut for the rich and business owners. The richest 1% will get a 61% of this tax cut versus the bottom two-thirds of American taxpayers, who will see just a 4% benefit.

In contrast to the huge tax cuts for the rich, the bill cut taxes for 69% of taxpayers from $75 to $2,200 a year on average. Not exactly enough to change a life. Did you know most items that benefit the middle-class start to expire in 2025?

Many rich people do not pay much in taxes, and some pay nothing at all. That is why the Alternative Minimum Tax (AMT) was made into law. However, the 2017 tax bill weakens the AMT and allows rich people to exempt more of their income from their taxes due.

Estate tax exemptions for those leaving money to their heirs. went from $11 million per couple to $22 million. While this tax bill helped rich people in the past, today, their exemption has doubled.

A New York Times article by Emmanuel Saez and Gabriel Zuckman shows that "the tax rate on the highest-income Americas was only 23% in 2018."

Trump's Tax Cuts and Jobs Act in 2017 should have been called the "Rich Americans and Corporations Tax Relief Act." Just as Trump promised that his Tax Cut and Jobs Act would spur businesses to grow with more and better-paying jobs, President Reagan made similar promises with this "trickle-down theory."

During his presidency, Reagan significantly increased public expenditures, primarily the Department of Defense. On the other hand, Reagan significantly reduced the maximum tax rate, which affected the highest income earners. He created the slowest rate of growth in inflation-adjusted spending since Eisenhower. The federal deficit as a percent of GDP was up throughout the Reagan presidency. The US borrowed both domestically and abroad to cover the Federal budget deficits, raising the national debt from $997 billion to $2.85 trillion. This led to the US moving from the world's largest international creditor to the world's largest debtor nation.

And true to form, The Trump Tax Cut and Jobs Act of 2017 put the United States far deeper into debt, just like Reagan did.

The National Debt is hard to comprehend. People rarely even talk about it anymore. But as of this writing, the yearly government shortfall of money is $3.6 trillion. The actual national debt is 28.4 trillion dollars. Imagine that you have a magic credit card, and you can spend, spend, spend, and they never cut off the credit. That is what has happened. We are a nation of people with a credit card addiction that is slowly choking the life out of our future generations. This addition is fed directly by an Overspending Congress and the greed of *Rich People, Big Businesses, and Corporations*.

Many people hate the IRS. But let's be clear, we need the IRS to collect money to pay the national bills. Congress makes the tax laws, not the IRS. The United States Congress continually attacks the IRS in public forums and in budget cuts. They fail to provide for the IRS's Mission. The Constitution grants Congress the right to tax. Currently, Congress uses Obama Care issues to stir up negative publicity for the IRS in order to protect their friends and business interests—the rich and greedy corporations. No government agency can be sustainable, let alone efficient if faced with yearly budget cuts, arcane budget keeping methods, a 63-year-old computer system, and increasingly complex tax laws. It was recently announced that the IRS expects 52,000 of its employees to leave or retire in the next six years. The IRS only has 83,000 employees

Conditions must change for the IRS. For this to happen, Congress must acknowledge that we have an unfair, unbalanced tax system that is a burden to all citizens because it does not seek to fairly and equitably apply the tax laws to all people. Shockingly, 14-20% of all adult citizens never file or pay taxes.

The more I write about this, the angrier I get. Did you know that there are three tax systems? One is for the W-2 wage earner employees trapped in a box and subject to the IRS sticking a hot poker in from time to time. A second system that benefits rich individuals. Finally, a third system that benefits corporations and other businesses that pay little or no corporate income taxes.

Who pays zero income taxes? Netflix, Amazon, Honeywell, Chevron, Delta Air, Eli Lilly, GM, Gannett News, Goodyear Tire and Rubber, Halliburton, IBM, Molson Coors, Jet Blue, US Steel, and Whirlpool! They made $79 billion in profits! This could have yielded $16 billion in taxes, but they followed the tax laws that they helped to write and essentially paid nothing at all.

The complex and confusing Internal Revenue Code is a problem created by Congress without the approval of the majority of Americans who voted them into office. When will the people of this country rise up and demand a fair and balanced tax system?

For sure, a broken tax system corrupted by political greed hurts all of us.

The IRS budget has been cut over and over by approximately 26% in real terms by both the Obama and Trump administrations. The IRS is crippled and weak and cannot keep up with a population that has grown by 15% from 2010 to 2020.

The IRS deserves credit for operating at all given its antiquated computer system, its aging employee population, the increasingly complex tax laws, advances in technology, electronic filing, and the budget cuts it has suffered for the last 12 years. Looking at how IRS is still operating is a remarkable feat; it is like watching a tired, old three-legged dog forced to go for an endless run.

My story, I am Richard Schickel, and I was an *IRS Senior Revenue Officer*/Tax Collector for 33 years. Once retired, I wanted to help people survive the great IRS dragon. To do so, I became an Enrolled Agent, a tax professional licensed by the IRS, and this license allows me to help people anywhere in the USA. I founded

RMS Tax Consulting LLC in Tucson, AZ, along with other retired IRS employees because I wanted to serve people in trouble with the IRS. I know how the IRS thinks and acts. I was a highly decorated foot soldier who did bad things for the IRS. Some of the things I did are not even legal to do now, but they were standard practice then.

Every day, I seized (levied) people's cash, bank accounts, assets, homes, cars, trucks, businesses, and anything else I could find and get my hands on. I was very good at being very bad. Now, I want to share strategies that will take away your fear and worry with the IRS. Now, I help people get the best deals that they can get from the IRS. Currently, the IRS is offering unheard of "deals" if you only know where to find them.

My whole life, I have been promoting and enforcing "voluntary tax compliance." That was really just another term for promoting fear as the system the IRS used to make sure taxpayers would fall into lockstep and file and pay their taxes. The IRS doesn't have the strength to do that today.

As a result of a crippled system, many people just stopped filing and paying their taxes. This idea spread as they tell their family, friends, and neighbors, and then even more people stopped paying taxes. This happened first in small towns far from the big cities where I worked as "the IRS guy." I would come into a town and make a big splash taking actions against prominent local citizens and others to "show them" that the IRS was powerful, mighty, and right in their backyard. My "boots on the ground" presence raised the "voluntary compliance" in the whole area for years to come. However, now that is all gone. No IRS agents even go to many of those towns anymore. Why? There is not enough staff and not enough money to travel.

The IRS can do an excellent job administering tax laws if funding is restored and increased. The IRS budget has been cut over and over by approximately 26% in real terms by both the Obama and Trump administrations.

It is not that the IRS can simply hire a bunch of people and then get back to work. Tax auditing and tax collection are amazingly complex. The IRS has not had a mass hiring for 12 years. In that time, a vast amount of institutional knowledge and experience has walked out of the door. Did you know that most technical positions require two or more years of on-the-job instruction before an employee becomes self-sufficient?

Over time, helping my clients has become my only focus. My goal is to get my clients the best deal that I can from the IRS.

Six years ago, I wrote two books, *IRS Whistleblower* and *What to Do When the IRS is After You—Secrets of the IRS*. These books are popular and explain how it was to be in the IRS when the IRS was robust, ruthless, and unrestrained. In my own Cassandra way as an author, I was warning Congress that the IRS needed more new employees, increased funding, new computers, and new powers to keep up with the US tax world of today.

My books were an accurate prophecy. What I predicted about the broken tax system has all come true.

Today, the IRS is at its weakest state in the last fifty years, and that can benefit you. The IRS has continued to decline. It is a broken vessel unable to carry on its mission of promoting a fair and effective tax system of audits and collections because Congress is acting irresponsibly.

At no time do I advocate non-filing or non-payment of your federal income or business tax obligations. This book tells you how to maneuver in the IRS system. The IRS, which was once somewhat fair and reasonable, now resembles a giant "clusterfuck." Today, the tax code is very lopsided and gives the rich and powerful people, especially those who are politically well connected, advantages that the rest of us don't have.

We all know that the United States Government must have money coming in regularly. Timely revenue pays the government's costs. The IRS collects approximately $3 trillion a year. Lately, our government is spending three times that amount, and the US debt is climbing each year. This is madness! And to make it worse, some businesses and individuals gain an unfair advantage because they get away with breaking tax laws. That unfair advantage means that they lower the price of their goods and services below the businesses that follow the law, which in turn drives the "good guys" out of business. The IRS knows who is breaking the law yet can do little or nothing about it.

These are the Facts:

- In 2019 at least 4,032,157 people and businesses did not file the required tax returns.
- 21,000,000 people and businesses did not pay their federal income and business taxes.
- Covid-19 was the only reason that the IRS re-started its *High-Income Non-Filer* (HINF) program because *Collection Field Revenue Collection Officers* could not go out to homes and businesses in person.
- The IRS has a *High-Income / High-Wealth* (HIHW) program to target non-filers and non-payors, but the program was stopped because the IRS did not have enough money or employees to work those cases.
- Some *High-Income / Non-Filer* cases that the IRS previously worked with became closed cases because the IRS was unable to contact or locate these citizens even though the IRS knew where they were when they earned money.
- The IRS knew that between 2014-2016 High-Income Non-Filers did not file or pay $45.7 billion in taxes. The IRS did nothing about it, and this egregious behavior continues.
- In 2019, the IRS let $6.7 billion in collectible tax debt expire and go away forever. This was an increase of 1,000% since 2010!

Here are some unpublished secrets of the IRS:

- Most IRS back taxes go away forever at the end of ten years.
- You should never file more than the last six years' delinquent tax returns. Not ever.
- Currently, the odds of your getting audited are low, so claim all of your income and expenses.
- You can practically write your own installment agreement terms for the first time with the IRS.

- You are probably not going to jail unless you owe the IRS huge bucks.

Let me show you how to:
- Write your own installment agreement.
- Never fully pay your back taxes due to financial hardship.
- Only pay part of your taxes but not suffer an IRS lien.
- Avoid the IRS *Offer-in-Compromise* program, which seldom works.
- To avoid bankruptcy which usually does not help you with your IRS problem.
- Chose a tax professional to help you at an IRS audit.
- Not trust most tax professionals who advertise in the media.

This book can protect your rights which the IRS sometimes forgets to tell you about. Reading this book can give you advantages that other delinquent taxpayer do not get. It can save your financial and emotional life.

Most people do not deliberately wake up one day and decide to mess with the IRS. These people experienced problems in their lives that were beyond their control. Maybe their business market changed, or their business model failed to keep up with a volatile market. Maybe they experienced Covid-19, death, divorce, drugs, drinking, depression, and a host of other things that can put a person off track in their lives. They did not pay the IRS for one reason or another.

These taxpayers need to be educated on what to do in the future. Taxpayers do not need to be made to feel like guilty criminals for the next ten years of their lives just because they owe the IRS money. Taxpayers need to be educated on how and what to do in the future. This book helps protect rights you have that IRS might forget to tell you about.

Acting on the secrets, policies, and procedures outlined in this book will save you worry, stress, and a whole lot of money in the future. So just keep reading and hang in here with me.

If you owe back taxes, this is the best time ever to owe the IRS. The book will show you strategies to get the best payment deals the IRS has ever offered. It will show you how to reduce or eliminate a majority of your tax burden in the future. It will show you how to avoid audits and what the IRS looks at as "tax crimes."

It does not matter if this is the first time you have owned the IRS or have owned back taxes for years. This book will help you find relief. If you have struggled to pay an installment agreement imposed by the IRS, I will show you how to get the lowest possible agreement, whether your taxes ever get paid off or not. Sometimes, if you prove that you are experiencing financial hardship, the IRS will agree not to collect any money from you for two to three years. Many people with financial hardships never pay off their IRS taxes, and that is O.K. with the IRS. The IRS is desperate for you to give them money, but the law does not allow them to crush you financially doing so. Although the intentional failure to pay Federal Income tax is a crime (Internal Revenue Code §7203), owing the IRS does not need to cost you your peace of mind. If you made mistakes in the past, I will show you a whole new world of tax forgiveness, tax deferral, and asset protection. You can benefit from the tax laws just like President Trump, and other *Rich People* have.

CHAPTER 2
HOW DID YOU GET IN TROUBLE WITH THE IRS?

Everyone agrees that taxes allow the United States to be a free and prosperous country. Taxes pay for schools, roads, military, government benefit programs, and these expenditures benefit everyone. Most people agree that we must have a sound tax system.

The public expects the IRS to enforce the tax laws fairly and justly. Most taxpayers believe that if they have to pay taxes, other taxpayers should also have to pay their "fair share" of taxes. Promoting tax compliance is something that taxpayers expect the IRS to monitor and encourage.

The Comprehensive Taxpayer Attitude Survey (CTAS) found that "95% of people agree that it is every American's civic duty to pay their fair share of taxes." And "87% believe that it is not at all acceptable to cheat on your taxes." A Gallup Poll said that of those people it surveyed, "69% said that corporations don't pay enough in taxes." Likewise, "62% said that the rich people do not pay their fair share of taxes either."

You may be reading this book because you are in trouble with the IRS. If so, it scares the hell out of you because receiving letters from the IRS telling you that you owe money or are being audited is like finding a winning ticket in a lottery after it has expired. You are special, but not in a good way!

Chapter 2: How Did You Get in Trouble with the IRS?

Mission Statement of the IRS

> *The Internal Revenue Service Collection Division promotes voluntary compliance. It collects delinquent taxes and secures delinquent tax returns through the fair and equitable application of the tax laws, including enforcement tools when appropriate. The collection program's mission also includes educating its customers to facilitate future tax compliance, thereby protecting and promoting public confidence in the American tax system.*

When IRS says "voluntary compliance," they mean it is voluntary—until you stop filing and paying taxes! Then, it is illegal. Failing to file an income tax return is a misdemeanor (one to three years). Let me emphasize the "enforcement tools" part of that mission sentence suggests "voluntary," which means quite the opposite? It means "voluntary" until you stop volunteering, and then it becomes urgent and mandatory. When the IRS calls your failure to file and pay taxes "intentional and affirmative," that will trigger the "tax evasion" label, and then you are looking at a felony. That's a sentence of 10-12 years!

Let's start at the very beginning—you did not file or pay your taxes because:

(check all that apply)

- I don't want to pay taxes.
- I need the money to support my family or extended family.
- I have COVID-19/health-related expenses, funeral expenses, or other medical expenses.
- I don't have the money to pay due to periods of unemployment.
- My friends stopped filing and paying and got away with it.
- I don't have any money or savings or assets.
- I don't believe that I will ever get Social Security.

- I think taxes are unfair or un-American.
- I needed the tax money for food, rent, or other expenses.
- I needed the money for my wedding, a vacation, or my new house.
- I needed the money to pay for recreational drugs, gambling, compulsive spending.

In my experience, most of the reasons that people owe taxes come down to bad choices, poor decisions, divorce proceedings, drugs, drinking, deceptive practices, adultery, gambling, greed, fraud, and deliberate tax evasion. Covid-19 is added to the list because the spread of the virus has resulted in lost work time, lost wages, destroyed businesses, evictions, foreclosures, medical bills, and funeral expenses.

Owing the IRS is scary. You might think that you can just call the IRS and make a deal. That rarely works, but you want to do the right thing. Do you think that you can just call them or go into a local IRS and tell them your circumstances, and then all will be right in your world again? Think again. The IRS only answers about 22% of the calls, and if they do, they will be friendly to you when you contact them and then use whatever reasons, excuses, or circumstances you claim against you.

Never call the IRS unless they are taking something from you right now. (i.e., *Levying/Seizing* your bank account or wages.

Never just go into an IRS office. The IRS requires that you make an appointment online, usually 4-6 weeks out. When you arrive at your appointment, you generally find people with sour dispositions who clearly could care less about helping you.

The IRS uses fear to mess with people, so today is your lucky day. My book will tell you what you need to know to take away your fear and show you a path out of the mess you are in. Owing the IRS is a life-changing experience and not a good one. Maybe you owe the IRS either accidentally or on purpose, and you have gotten caught. If you made false claims on your tax return because you did not understand the law or made a math error is one thing and is simple to resolve. Still, because people enjoy the rewards of their work—people enjoy the money and the power that money brings. Your ego says, "It's my money. I earned it. I want to keep it all." The IRS disagrees, and that is when your tax problems start.

When the IRS letters begin to arrive, your problems multiply if you do not immediately open them, read them and act on what they tell you to do. You must open the letters! Because the IRS is giving you the right to appeal, these rights are time-sensitive and quickly go away.

Many people have excuses not to open IRS letters. Some say: "I'm too busy," or "I'm too afraid to open IRS letters." People are so overwhelmed with their daily lives that they try to evade the truth. They feel frustrated and harassed by life, blaming their tax problems on Covid-19, the economy, their business market, their competitors, their partners, their spouse, their employees, the President, Congress, and the IRS. But in the end, it is just you and the IRS.

Are You a Delinquent Taxpayer?

The way the IRS sees it, you had the income, and the tax money went through your hands, and they feel you spent it for something other than paying your taxes. The IRS already has a negative impression of you before you even contact them. They call people who do not file or pay "delinquent taxpayers." The word "delinquent" means a person who is an offender, or guilty, or embroiled in a situation that is bad.

However, the IRS has no right to make you feel shame, dishonor, worry, fear, and anger just because you did not pay your taxes.

Remember, knowledge is power. I will show you how to get a fair evaluation of your current financial situation and an arrangement to address your taxes that will benefit you and the IRS. More importantly, just because you had the money for taxes does not mean that there is any money left. The IRS can't collect money from you that you don't have.

The IRS is not just looking for its taxes; it is also punishing you every month with a compounded daily interest charge. Plus, there is the "failure to file penalty" (up to 25%) and "failure to pay penalty" (up to 25%). So, add it all up; you owe more in penalties and interest over the years than you ever owed in taxes.

You need to know how to stand up for yourself and do your best to make payment arrangements. You need to show the IRS why you cannot make payments now or maybe never into the future. With COVID-19, depression, death, and economic collapse, the money you owe the IRS is probably the least of your problems. Whether you ever fully pay your taxes is not your problem; it's a problem for the IRS. Think of it this way, whether you owe $10,000 or $10 million, if you don't have it, you don't have it. This is where I come in. I will reveal how to get the best deal that IRS has available, whether they advertise it or not.

The US Economy and You in 2021 and 2022

The economy was not in good shape for working people before Covid-19 came into our world. Also, we can expect that some jobs are just never coming back. This has resulted in a massive number of unemployed (12.6 million people). 12.6 million is the combined population of New York City and Los Angeles!

Due to Covid-19, there is a tremendous financial reorganization taking place. Most everyone will be affected by the changes. Here's what happens when people run short of money. They "borrow" from the IRS, believing they can easily pay it back later. This belief will be poisoning our economy for at least the next five years. Continuing financial uncertainty will also affect any ability to make payment agreements with the IRS. Yet, the IRS believes all citizens must pay taxes regardless of their circumstances.

How to Resolve Your Case

Every IRS case can be resolved in one of the following ways:

- Full payment by the taxpayer or from levy/seizure of wages, salary, otherincome, bank accounts, or other assets or sale of assets.
- An *Installment Agreement* (IA)

- *Currently Not Collectible* Status due to financial hardship (i.e., You cannot pay your taxes at all at the present time. This is a deferment or suspension of tax collection activity. You still owe the money. See Chapter 11.
- *Offer in Compromise/Settlement Agreement*—sadly, this is frequentlyadvertised by sleazy tax firms in the media and is rarely accepted by the IRS.
- Bankruptcy.
- Appeals or Audit or Tax Court to reduce or remove the tax.
- Innocent Spouse or Injured Spouse tax reduction or relief.
- Death of taxpayer.
- The case will be *Shelved*. The case will sit on the IRS shelf untouched , possibly forever.
- The case will be in the *Queue*. This is a holding place waiting for an IRS employee to become available to work it.
- The case will be *Tolerance*. This means the balance due is too small for the IRS to go after.
- Tax *balances will expire* due to the expiration of the Statute of Limitations of IRS Collections—which is ten years after the taxes were assessed.

Guess what? If you have an *Installment Agreement* (IA) or you case is in *Currently Not Collectible* status, as long as you continue to file and pay your current taxes and have filed them for the last six years, your case will just sit where it is currently in the IRS system.

What is the Problem?

A lot of people stop filing. The reasons are similar as to why they do not pay. Everyone has a reason. The IRS acknowledges that millions of people have not filed tax returns. The number is probably closer to four million or more per year because the IRS applies various filters that tell the agency that if the unfiled tax returns will yield less than $10,000 or less than $1,000, it is not worth it for them to spend any time getting the return. Because some returns will result in a refund, they do not usually try to get those returns.

Now, imagine that every person in the city of Chicago, Houston, or Seattle just stopped filing a tax return; then you can envision just how many unfiled tax returns there are. There are currently 2,291,000 unfiled tax returns, which the IRS calls "delinquent return investigations." These are active open investigations. But that does not mean that there is anyone in the IRS looking at them or working them.

IRS collection is unable to promote voluntary filing compliance because currently, it lacks a physical presence in small and medium-sized towns across the United States. The IRS admits that the actual voluntary compliance rate is only 84%, which is probably overstated. Think of it this way. In a crowd of 100 people, 16 are probably not filing or paying any taxes! But there is you, the good citizen currently reading this tax book who does pay your taxes usually.

Some taxpayers think that the IRS has just "gone away." The IRS may lack employees, but the IRS has not gone away. The IRS usually sends two letters asking for a delinquent tax return. If they do not hear from the taxpayer, they often close the investigation. In the majority of cases, the IRS doesn't get a tax return because of the lack of money in the agency's budget to follow up.

Some taxpayers have stopped filing and paying their taxes, thinking that if they don't bother the IRS, the IRS won't bother them. They think they can just drop out of the tax system. This is happening more and more.

As was previously mentioned, the budget cuts by Congress have crippled the IRS field presence. It is so severely stressed, due to fewer employees, that some zip codes in the United States are not being serviced at all. As a result, tax compliance suffers, and so does the US budget. These are the states where tax compliance and IRS staffing is the greatest:

- Arizona
- California

- Colorado
- Connecticut
- Florida
- Illinois
- New Jersey
- New York
- Oregon
- Pennsylvania
- Washington

Surprisingly some states still have a handful of IRS employees left. In fact, as I write this, the State of Alaska has only one revenue officer left.

Who Does Not Pay?

For the year 2016–13.1 million people did not pay their taxes. How many people is that? It is equivalent to every single person just stopped filing their taxes in the cities of Los Angeles, Houston, Phoenix, Philadelphia, San Antonio, San Diego, and Dallas. They just stopped and the IRS barely noticed. Add to that every year there are about 8 million new people who do not file their tax returns. In 2016, those people owed the IRS $421.8 billion at the end of the fiscal year. Add $150 million to that number every year. Today the IRS accounts receivable is closer to 1 trillion dollars. 13.1 million people already owed taxes plus 7.9 million new cases every year. Another way to look at the tax loss of $421.8 billion is that it is enough money to restore all the highways and bridges in the USA—many of which are 50 years old or more and dangerously falling apart.

In 2020, the IRS will fail to collect more than $630 billion, or nearly 15% of tax liabilities due. The government acknowledges this. Based on my 40 years in the tax field, the amount is probably closer to $1 trillion a year. This is from people who do not report their income or underreport it. Think of this in your own life. How many people do you know who you think are not reporting their income? They could be friends, neighbors, relatives, or people living at a higher standard of living than you. You know who they are; they flash their wealth in visible ways. I once had a cleaning lady driving a $67,000 vehicle that was fully paid for. She proudly told me that she had never paid taxes!

Despite the threat of owing thousands of dollars to the US government, millions of Americans continue to fall behind on their taxes. Every year the balance due grows larger and larger. Yet, Congress has manipulated the tax laws for the *Rich People, Big Businesses, and Corporations*. So, who is watching out for you?

As I will explain in a later chapter, that taxes are only due for ten years from the date the IRS says they are due. After ten years, that tax due expires and goes away. This is good news for you if you owe back taxes, and this book will explore how to increase the odds of that happening in your case. It is not good news for the IRS.

The IRS estimates that 15% of all taxes owed go unpaid annually. This "tax gap" could amount to $7.5 trillion over the next ten years. The IRS knows exactly who these people are but does nothing because Congress over the last 20 years has made the IRS powerless to collect those taxes due to the United States Treasury.

There is an estimated $2 trillion underground economy that is not filing or paying taxes. This would yield $700 billion in additional tax revenues a year. This income can be from legal or illegal sources such as prostitution, gambling (yes, your football pool is all taxable), drug sales, bribes, or crimes. The Internal Revenue Code does not care if your income is legal or illegal. All income is taxable. If you rob a bank, then the amount you took was taxable income.

Many businesses and self-employed people use the IRS as a lender; they just hold the money and hope to deal with their taxes later.

If You Are Unable to Fully Pay Your Taxes

The Internal Revenue Code does have exceptions for financial hardship situations. The Internal Revenue Manual (IRM) provides procedures for their employees that cases are to be reviewed with "heavy reliance on discretion, judgment, and experience." However, the IRS procedures do everything to discourage the IRS employees from applying this authority.

Many people in the IRS are new and lack experience and judgment skills. They cannot comprehend the powers their positions give them. However, if you cannot advocate for yourself and cannot prepare forms and financial statements required by the IRS, you can expect bad results. The IRS will plod along like a hungry bulldozer gobbling up your assets and destroying your life without regard to ethical correctness. Its job is to collect taxes.

Why Don't People Have Enough Money to Pay Their Taxes?

> *Some 90 percent of American workers have seen their incomes stagnate or decline in the past 30 years.*
> —Joseph Stiglitz, Economist, 2001 Nobel Prize Winner in Economics

In the past, I have collected taxes from thousands of people who have been financially very successful and then run into problems due to poor choices. Today, I work with people who don't make enough money to live on. Taxpayers are stretched so tight money-wise that they do not have enough money for the basics. At all levels, they are being squeezed; many people have no home equity, stocks, bonds, or savings. They are highly leveraged out with high rent and mortgage payments and necessary auto loans and student loans, so they cannot envision a time when they aren't in a financial crisis. A critical reason for this crisis stems from the lack of a living wage owed to workers, with companies paying less and less for work at all levels. That is why Economist Paul Krugman wrote: "Wages for ordinary workers have been stagnant since 1974." In 2011, Stiglitz wrote: "All the growth in recent decades—and more—has gone to those at the top."

Today there are 630 *billionaires* and over 1.5 million people worth more than $10 million in the United States. Economics is complex, but you know this yourself when you look at your finances every month. To prove this, you know that your income is much more than your parents or grandparents ever made but do you have as much cash, home equity, savings, stocks, and economic security as your parents? Probably not. Clearly, they could buy a lot more with a $20 bill in 1980 than you can now.

Also, households have changed. Fewer people are married. There are more single-parent homes, more children under eighteen, more childcare expenses, along with a need for computers, cell phones, internet expenses, and car payments that can go on for years into the future. Although wages went up, inflation took away any actual buying power.

Rich People, Big Businesses and *Corporations* argue that "a rising tide lifts all ships." It certainly lifts their yachts, but your boat is firmly tied to the dock, and now you are underwater.

Keep reading before you go down with your ship!

CHAPTER 3
POST-TRAUMATIC IRS DISORDER—THE PANDEMIC'S EFFECT ON THE IRS AND THE CHAOS THAT AWAITS

Today is the best time ever to owe the IRS because it is offering unusually liberal payment plans, and its tax enforcement is surprisingly lax.

The IRS budget doesn't provide enough staff, money, or computer power to keep up with the challenges of collecting taxes. The agency is harassing lower- and middle-class workers. Any tax audit or collection work on *Rich People, Big Businesses, and Corporations* are set aside with the claim that the agency does not have the money or the staff to work the complex issues big-dollar cases pose.

The IRS has been in a continual state of decline for the last twelve years as resources and brainpower keep walking out the door.

Here are the facts. In the past 30 years, while our population has increased, the IRS lost 38% of its employees! Shockingly the IRS had 116,673 employees in 1990 and now has 68,963 full-time employees. (83,000 employees with part-time and temporary employees.)

The number of IRS employees who work on the most complex examinations and collection matters declined, according to a July 2020 report from the Congressional Budget Office. From 2010 to

2019, the number of IRS *Revenue Agents* declined 35 percent, and *Collection Revenue Officers* dropped by a staggering 48%.

The IRS announced on July 6, 2021 that they would be hiring 1,300 new Revenue Agents and 700 Revenue Officers in Fall, 2021.

In the next six years, 52,000 employees are expected to retire or leave, according to Tony Reardon, President of the National Treasury Employees Union. Year after year, the IRS budget has been cut. There is no significant new hiring—furthermore, the IRS Master File computer celebrates its 63rd birthday this year. The oldest computer system in the federal government. The programming language is no longer taught in schools. **Think about that for a minute—the IRS computer system, if it were a person, would almost be eligible for Social Security benefits.**

Pity the IRS! This is not a new problem and has been orchestrated by *Rich People, Big Businesses, and Corporations.* How? Their connections with members of Congress for decades have provided the necessary loopholes for lost taxes.

For the past 75 years, the IRS has had a system for reaching most people who should be filing and paying taxes. Yet, when budget money dried up, and their workforce retired, the system continued to target poor W-2 wage-earners and small businesses. They will issue threats and try to intimidate people. It's all bark and little bite. FEAR is their friend. Fear controls and hurts people. My philosophy is, "FUCK FEAR!"

Here is a statement by IRS Commissioner Chuck Rettig, April 2021:

> The IRS understands that many taxpayers face challenges, and we're working hard to help people facing issues paying their tax bills; following up on our People First Initiative earlier this year, this next phase of our efforts will help with further taxpayer relief efforts.

Traditionally the IRS is not known for its understanding and compassion for the American taxpayer. Thus, it is very unusual for an IRS commissioner to make a friendly statement such as this.

Forget about a kinder, gentler IRS. The Golden Key to the IRS is available once you start paying your taxes. You start filing and paying your taxes right now for this year and continue to do so for the future. That puts you in the best position to negotiate any deals with the IRS.

If you surveyed taxpayers regarding their thought about taxes and their government in 2020, they might positively respond. They got more money back than they had paid in. That continues in 2021 due to Covid-19. If you survey tax preparers and tax professionals, that will tell you both years were endless nightmares, which continue to this day. Why is this? It's great that people received Economic Stimulus money and Economic Impact Grants, and Payroll Protection Program loans. It's just hard on the agency to administer the tax system when Congress keeps changing the tax code even after the tax year is over.

As I write this, the third stimulus payment was just approved and is on its way to millions of Americans. You can see the problem for tax professionals.

How the IRS Sees You

The IRS strategy is to see delinquent taxpayers as shameless. I have witnessed how IRS agents will deliberately be stirring up guilt, fear, and shame in delinquent taxpayers. As a result, they promote a policy that makes people feel like dirt. The IRS cannot sustain this threatening model any longer because it has no foot soldiers left. Think of the Wizard of Oz. When the curtain is pulled back, there is just a tired old man madly pulling the levers creating terror for everyone. That's the current IRS position—a tired old man.

Recently the IRS gave an automatic extension to all individuals delaying the filing date until July 15, 2020, because of Covid-19. However, most people neither asked for nor wanted that extension. Sitting at home with nothing to do but stare at their walls, they had their tax information. This extension stripped them of the urgency of preparing them or at least dropping the information off with their tax preparer. Clearly, the IRS is insensitive and tone-deaf to its taxpayers and places tax preparers in an awkward position timewise.

This extension led to the most extended tax season in history for many tax preparers. Some taxpayers even filed a further extension until October 15, 2020. It was a year that will be the last for many senior tax preparers because it was an absolute mess, and they quit the business.

Most tax professionals received hundreds of calls about the *Economic Injury Disaster Loans* (EIDL) and *Payroll Protection Program* (PPP) grants and loans. Without the credentials and training, tax preparers had no business offering advice. But tax people are quick on their feet, so they help out. As a result of some potentially inaccurate advice, there could be ramification for the government and taxpayer.

Hundreds of thousands of businesses are closing daily as I write this; they don't have the funds to continue. In some cases, the government gave them the PPP loans, which were to be used for rent and payroll, but many of them were not legally able to open their businesses due to the Covid-19 mandates. These loans did them no good at all for their business, but desperate times called for desperate measures, and they kept the money. I know many loans were labeled excessive and most probably were fraudulent.

How did Covid-19 affect taxpayers?

- They lost income tax return-average refunds of $3,000.
- They didn't know that all unemployment income is taxable; furthermore, most people had no withholding taxes taken out.
- Their hopes were dashed because remote working expenses are not deductible.
- They also discovered home office deductions do not apply to wage earners as a tax deduction.
- The taxpayer moved to find another job but found moving expenses are not deductible.
- If your company tells you to move, this relocation money is taxable.

- It increased tax liabilities to other States where work was done. For example: if you moved from California to Texas, you had to pay taxes in both states.
- Millions will lose their *Earned Income Tax Credit* monies resulting in $2-7 thousand loss to the taxpayers.
- Although the IRS forgives taxes on PPP loans—state taxes will apply in AZ, CA, CT, FL, ID, KY, ME, MN, NC, NH, NV, OH, TX, UT, VA, VT, WA.

The Loss of Earned Income Credit (EITC) Will Affect Millions

Many working parents qualify for this *Earned Income Tax Credit*. As the name implies, to be eligible for the *Earned Income Credit*, you must "earn" income, either as an employee or as a self-employed person. However, receiving unemployment benefits doesn't mean you're automatically ineligible for the credit. There are other requirements you'll also need to satisfy to claim the EITC. If you do, the credit can reduce your taxes or even create a refund. For many of my clients receiving $10,000 in unemployment, it reduced their EITC by $3,000. For some in 2020, with their much-reduced incomes, this eliminated the EITC refunds because unemployment income does not count as wage income.

Unemployment Benefits—Mixed Blessings

A curious combination of unemployment reimbursements in various states had some unemployed people bringing home more money from unemployment than they would have earned from working at their regular job. However, not only will they lose the earned income credit, but they will also lose whatever tax refund they would usually get. How can this be? Here is an example: The average IRS tax refund is $2,781.00. Unemployment with the federal supplemental payment of $600 a week for the time offered and with three children, the wage earner would receive almost $10,000. I spoke to one man who made $1,456.00 a week for 39 weeks. He earned $56,784. However, with less exemptions and deductions, he owed about $6,000 on income taxes and late payment penalties. He didn't know he needed to pay taxes on unemployment monies.

In Montana, New Mexico, and Oklahoma, the average person's unemployment checks were 170% of what they would have been able to earn. Unemployed people got 160% of what they would have earned in Oregon, South Dakota, Iowa, Kentucky, West Virginia, Delaware, North Carolina, Mississippi, and Georgia.

This is lucky for them until they file their tax returns only to find they owe taxes because, unlike a paycheck with a tax withdrawal made in advance, they used all their money from the unemployment check for living expenses. At this time, not only does the unemployed worker owe tax money, but they are still unemployed.

401k and IRA Distributions

Because of Covid-19, people were allowed to borrow up to 100% of their 401k or IRA value. The clincher is they must repay it within three years. Here are the details.

Congress passed the CARES Act (Coronavirus Aid, Relief and Economic Security Act), which allows people to take penalty-free retirement plan distributions up to $100,000 in 2020 and have three years to either pay it back or pay the tax on the distribution. Some businesses will advance a loan based on your 401k while exacting a 10% penalty applied to the total loan if you don't pay it back. However, if the employee can't pay it back, the distribution then becomes fully taxable. Sadly, a large percentage of people probably will be unable to because they will lose their jobs or the company will go out of business. If they can pay it back, then they must file an amended tax return. This will be great for tax preparers like me because we make money on extra work, but this is a hardship and extra cost for many people who have been hit hard by Covid-19. Additionally, if the taxpayer has to claim the Covid-19 distribution as income, they will have unexpected tax bills on top of the potential 401k withdrawal. This will be a real mess.

Chapter 3: Post-Traumatic IRS Disorder—The Pandemic's Effect on the IRS . . .

Taxpayer Relief Initiative (TRI). What is the TRI?

The IRS announced a new program, the *Taxpayer Relief Initiative*, to help taxpayers unable to pay their taxes because of the pandemic. (If you are interested, do a Google search on "IR-2020-248"). Taxpayers who owe taxes and cannot pay have always had options such as *Installment Agreements* and *Offer-in-Compromise*, but now they have more options:

- Taxpayers who qualify for the short-term payment plan option now have up to 180 days to resolve their tax liabilities instead of the usual 120 days.
- The IRS says it will offer more flexibility for taxpayers who are temporarily unable to meet the payment terms of an accepted *Offer in Compromise*. (How do they do this?)
- *Installment Agreement* options are available for taxpayers who can pay their balance over time. The IRS *Expanded Installment Agreement* removes the requirement for financial statements and substantiation where balances owed are less than $250,000 if the monthly payment proposal is sufficient. This type of agreement continues until the tax is paid or the CSED is expired (*Collection Statute of Expirations*), and the tax goes away forever.
- The IRS will automatically add any new tax balances to your existing installment. This will occur even if you default on your previous IRS CSED agreement.
- Some individual taxpayers who haven't paid 2019 taxes and owe less than $250,000 may qualify to set up an installment agreement without having a *Notice of Federal Tax Lien* filed by the IRS. A *Notice of Federal Tax Lien* means the IRS will file a lien against any real and/or personal property in public records. Your credit is ruined. This is another major secret that the IRS does not share.
- Qualified taxpayers with an existing *Direct Debit Installment Agreements* may now be able to use the

online payment agreement system to propose lower monthly payment amounts and change their payment due dates. https://www.irs.gov/payments/online-payment-agreement-application. Currently, the IRS has not published who or what qualifies a taxpayer for this *Direct Debit Installment Agreement*. Why not?

- Taxpayers who cannot pay can contact the IRS to request a temporary halt in collection efforts, which the IRS will grant if the taxpayer is currently unable to pay. The IRS determines if you can't pay from the financial statements that you provide.

- Existing *installment agreements* had direct debits suspended from April to July 2020. Some have not started back up as of July 2021. This seems like a good thing, but there is an emotional toll due to the anxiety of payments hanging over taxpayer's heads.

- If you miss an *installment agreement* payment because you could not send a check or pay online, then the IRS provides an "automatic skip" once in every agreement. There is talk that IRS may provide an automatic skip for their delinquent accounts once a year.

- More liberal penalty relief, *Reasonable Cause for Penalty Relief*, is discussed more in Chapter 11.

- *Offer in Compromise*—Certain taxpayers qualify to settle their tax bill for less than the amount they owe by submitting an *Offer in Compromise*. To help determine eligibility, use the *Offer in Compromise Pre-Qualifier Tool* (Google). The IRS can offer additional flexibility for some taxpayers who are temporarily unable to meet the payment terms of an accepted *Offer in Compromise* depending on the circumstance.

- For the wage earner, IRS stopped all enforced collection activity for ten months in 2020.

Let me tell you, these are nice words, but the agency doesn't tell you how to get the deals bulleted above. The IRS likes to keeps its controlling position through information management.

The more you can know about the Covid-19 provisions and the IRS's crippled state, the more it will benefit you.

Continue reading to find out exactly how.

Do not fall into Post Traumatic IRS Disorder.

CHAPTER 4

HOW DIFFERENTLY DOES THE IRS TREAT RICH PEOPLE, BIG BUSINESSES, CORPORATIONS, AND YOU?

Rich People, Big Businesses, and Corporations can hire tax professionals like me (Enrolled Agents, CPA's or tax attorneys) to protect their interests. Congress has been generous in writing tax codes to protect those citizens who seem to manipulate the tax laws that other people must follow. If you are reading this book, you fall into the latter category. You're on your own.

The Tax Code is riddled with tax benefits for *Rich People, Big Businesses, and Corporations* but not for the blue-collar and the middle classes who are the backbone of the United States socially and economically. The IRS system could be operated differently and better. I will offer my recommendations in a later chapter. However, you need to deal with the current system.

Thanks to the Trump-approved Tax Cut & Jobs Act of 2017, corporations pay 21% in taxes. From 1960 on the percentage kept dropping from 52% to 35% and is now 21%. That computes to a 40% drop in the business tax rate. "In the 1950s, '60s, and '70s, many corporations paid about half of their profits to the federal government. Although all income taxes were reduced, the *Rich People* got most of the benefits. Many years ago, the top tax rate for "the top 1%" was 90%. Before the Trump Tax Cut & Jobs Act of 2017, the tax rate had been lowered to 39.6%, and today it is 37%. The tax rate only dropped 2.6%, yet, with the 2017 program, business tax rate reduction was 40%. You can see how the Trump Tax Cut and Jobs Act of 2017 favored corporations.

Wise *Rich People* now keep their money in their corporation/business accounts and accumulate tax-free equity with their business assets. While the tax cuts signed by President Trump did help *Rich People* at this level, however, they didn't do much for you. You used to be able to deduct buying a house, making a charitable donation, get a benefit when you have more than two kids and a host of other deductions. Congress wiped out all beneficial tax deductions to the middle and lower classes. Worse than that, whatever 2.6% tax cut was given will expire by 2025, and individuals' tax rates will go up again.

Determining income and wealth is not easy. Most people make more money than they did ten years ago because they are paid higher wages, but everyone knows that since 1980 the value of that money has decreased. You're making more money, but not enough to buy all that you need.

The inflation rate since 1980 is 240%. In simple terms, that means that what you could buy for $100 in 1980 now costs $340. Plus, you have expenses that many people did not have in 1980. One example is child-care (more mothers have to work to afford a middle-class lifestyle). Our society demands the following: cell phones, computers, internet-connect fees, cable or Netflix type bills, to name a few expenses. Plus, higher taxes have been passed on cigarettes, alcohol, gas, food, and even sales tax. People put other expenses on credit cards that were not widely available in 1980. Once you don't pay the credit card bill, interest as high as 18-29% will be added to your financial burden. This vicious cycle is continually sucking up the money that working people make. You need a lot more money to survive economically.

Who is Rich, and Who is Poor?

How much money you make and how much your assets are worth will determine how you interpret this next section. Which income category are you in now that Covid-19 is here?

There are six groups of people in the United States.

Poor or near-poor	$32,048 or less
Lower-middle class	$32,048–$53,413
Middle class	$53,413–$106,827
Upper-middle class	$106,827–$373,894
Rich	$373,894 and up
Ultra-rich	Worth over $30 million

Based on income for a family of 3 people

Income categories depend on: where you live, the cost of living, and your lifestyle. For example, a 2-bedroom condo in Tucson, Arizona, might be $250,000, whereas a comparable condo in San Francisco might be $2 million.

Do you have enough money in your bank account to pay an emergency $400 payment? This means the money must be in your savings account, not a credit advance you could get on a credit card. 40% of households said that they did not have that much money. The likely reason is the high cost of living and the high expectations that business advertising has planted in our heads about "how" we should live. Shows like the Kardashians encourage people to spend money like they have as much money as movie stars. You're paying for a visible fix that cannot be sustained. It's a type of mental programming. People don't pay taxes because the money that should be dedicated to the IRS funds their fantasies.

IRS Anger

There is a lot of anger directed at the Internal Revenue Service. Many people feel that they are being squeezed out of existence with taxes. This list is long: the 10 million people unemployed (30% of them unemployed for a year or more.) Covid-19, the failing economy, and the loss of manufacturing jobs. I could feel the anger and frustration as people attended Trump rallies and invaded the US Capitol on January 6th. A percentage of Americans think that the current political and economic systems have passed them by.

But remember, Congress is where all laws are created. Educate yourself on how the US system works so that your vote will represent you in the US Congress by educating, lobbying, and networking even with people that you don't necessarily like. Appealing for other voters to support the people who support what you want is an essential step too.

Finding candidates that present information regarding what you believe tax laws should look like is how to make positive change. That is what the *Rich People, Big Businesses, and Corporations* have learned to do, and it has paid off in a big way for them.

It is essential to know how the IRS thinks and why it does what it does. It can be difficult to understand how tax laws weave together, internal revenue procedures, court rulings, letter rulings, and dozens of other rules and laws that are confusing to taxpayers. The IRS bureaucracy is over-concerned with procedures at the expense of common sense. I can also add that the IRS employees are distrustful and paranoid. Their experience makes them see dark shadows behind every taxpayer. The IRS is happy to see itself as the *Accuser*, the *Cop*, the *Judge*, the *Jury*, and the *Jailer*.

For instance, in the Social Security program, all employers and employees pay the 15.3% required for Social Security and Medicare. That means on an income up to $142,800; this adds up to $21,848. Currently, if a person had wages of $1 million, they will not pay on any amount over the $142,800. If they paid 15.3% on their $1 million, they would have to pay an additional $131,152. This equitable approach would make the Social Security Trust fund secure for the next 50 years!

In 2019, there was a big blow-up about President Donald Trump's taxes. He is a real estate developer, and that industry is where income taxes can be deferred years into the future. That is legal. Income-producing properties that are probably gaining in value can, under the tax laws, be depreciated. This is my example: A business buys a building or a machine, and the tax laws claim that it loses its value over time even though the machine might still remain highly functioning. It is not worthless after a year or five or seven years.

The adjustment of retirement age has a cost. A person who labors for a living in a physically demanding job and who is getting old and not as strong has no tax option for depreciating their body. They cannot depreciate themselves as they could a property, a machine, or other business assets.

You have little or nothing. The economy of the last 20 years combined with Covid-19 is crushing most working people. If the IRS is looking at you, you are probably terrified, maybe belligerent, and wonder why the IRS likes to pick on a poor working person like you.

Leona Helmsley famously said, "Only the little people pay taxes." More recently, Donald Trump made it clear to all Americans that paying taxes was unnecessary for wealthy individuals and businesses. He did this by slashing taxes on the rich and corporations and through his own personal example of manipulation of his own returns to avoid paying taxes. "When the little people see the big people not paying their fair share, it shatters the social contract and the concept of general welfare enshrined in the Constitution," Michael E. Mahler, Los Angeles, *NYT*- Letter to the Editor.

That is how the tax laws work. The IRS is unwilling to use its remaining resources to get *Rich People, Big Businesses, and Corporations* to file and pay taxes, so IRS just leans on you, the person who did file but cannot pay their taxes. It is not fair and equitable.

The media has revealed that Mr. Trump appears to have had an extraordinary amount of expenses in his businesses and little positive income (cash) actually to pay his bills, and perhaps that is why his tax returns are of such interest to the IRS. A historical fact was the tax evasion of the famous gangster Al Capone. The IRS put him in jail for his crimes of tax evasion.

Clearly, tax laws benefit *Rich People, Big Businesses, and Corporations* more than those working for a wage or even smaller self-employed people and their businesses. A further example of tax laws for the *Rich People*: much of the income for *Rich People* is not considered "taxable income by the IRS" This means that they have assets such as rental properties and stocks that are worth more and more every year, but if they do not sell them, then they do not pay taxes on the increase in their value. If *Rich People* never cash in their stocks or properties, the wealth transfer to their heirs. occurs without ever paying capital gains taxes on the increase in their value.

Working people have to report their income earned in the year that they earn it.

Some *Rich People* do pay taxes on their earned income. Look at Larry Ellison, the founder of Amazon. His salary is $81,840.

Ellison pays taxes on that. He does not receive any more stock as compensation, but then he does not need to. He already owns 53% of the company. That stock is worth $180 billion. Most of this money he has never paid any capital gains taxes on.

Steven Jobs, the founder of Apple, earned $1 a year. He borrowed money against the value of his stock, so that was a loan (loans are not taxable income), and then when he died, he passed his stock along to his heirs. and never paid any income or capital gains taxes on it either. At the time of his death, his stock was worth $10 billion.

Even many *Rich People* would agree that they pay too little in taxes. Warren Buffett said that his tax rate was less than any of the 20 people in his office. His secretary pays more (percentage-wise) than he does.

Rich People will pay 3.2% of their wealth in taxes (in theory) this year compared with 7.2% paid by the bottom 99 percent.

Also, 2,020 wealthy Americans will inherit $764 billion but pay only 2.1% on that money in inheritance taxes. To put this into perspective, in Great Britain, the inheritance tax is 40%.

In serving the interest of the wealthy sector, the Trump tax cuts canceled $1.7 trillion in taxes for 630 *billionaires* but did not cancel the $1.7 trillion in student loan debt for the 45 million Americans who owe it. Additionally, while in 2016, there were 353,402 high-dollar cases sitting in the *Collection Field (Revenue Officer Queue)* that were unlikely ever to be worked by a human being. So, these *Rich People* will never pay their fair share of taxes.

A few hundred wealthy tax evaders did not file tax returns from 2014 to 2016 on $10 billion in income, and the IRS knew about it and did not have the budget or employees to pursue it.

In the case of Trump, he is one example of how the ultra-wealthy and giant corporations pay no taxes. He avoided many of the taxes while using current tax laws. This is typical of real estate developers. The media disclosed that Trump reported no actual income, and he wrote off everything by charging expenses to his 500 businesses. He essentially paid no taxes.

It is true that in the 50 years since President Ronald Reagan came up with his "trickle-down" economic theory, sadly, very little money has trickled down to the middle class. The millionaires turned into billionaires, and the working class turned into the working poor.

Some people find that they owe taxes when they file their tax returns. In 2021 when people filed their tax returns for 2020, and because of unemployment income, they owed taxes. In many cases, they were used to receiving $2,000 to $7,000 for *Earned Income Tax Credit* Refund. But because they were not working, they had no refund tax check.

The IRS is so busy demanding money, scaring, and intimidating people that they often neglect or refuse to ask if taxpayers can pay what is owed in part or whole.

By the way, many anxious or intimidated taxpayers, seeking to resolve their liabilities as quickly as possible, are *unaware* that IRS is required to halt collections if the taxpayer is experiencing economic hardship. As a result, they agree to payments that they cannot afford. The lack of transparency in the IRS taxpayer relationship is abusive. And still, some people get away with not filing or reporting income or paying taxes due on millions of dollars. It is unfair to attack those at the bottom of the economy. The IRS can systemically identify all the people who are unable to pay.

If you are not aware of your rights and how to handle the IRS, you can be sure that IRS will "manhandle" you. This attitude never works out for the IRS in the long run because these actions make people resent the IRS and those taxpayers want some measure of justice. Oftentimes this resentment translates into unpaid taxes.

Millions of individuals, parents with children, and millions of children can lift themselves out of poverty. How? With the *Earned Income Tax Credit* (EITC), which helps vulnerable, needy individuals—"the working poor." Poor people (25 million) can claim the

Earned Income Tax Credit. The IRS audits 300,000 poor people a year for this EITC. The taxpayer error rate is 25% because of lack of education, improper payments, or fraudulent claims. This costs the US $17 billion a year in lost taxes.

Although the IRS is required to identify taxpayers who are at risk for economic hardship, they do not publish this information, but the taxpayer has the right to say that they cannot afford to pay the taxes due to reduced income or chronic unemployment. The IRS is then supposed to take a collection financial statement that will give the taxpayers a certain minimum standard of living with allowances for what they call "reasonable expenses" and then apply it across the board. The premise is that each taxpayer should have an adequate means to provide for basic living expenses. (See Chapter 11.)

Today it would be one thing if the IRS fairly administered the tax laws, but it does not. Sadly, poor people are more likely to be audited than *Rich People.* People owing under $50,000 in taxes are likely to be more aggressively collected than a person who owes over $1 million in taxes.

Notably, "the audit rate for the "top 1%" is only 0.5% while the middle—and lower-class audit rate is 25%.

The poverty line in the USA is $25,100 for a family of four. The median (middle) family income is only $59,000 for a family of four. As mentioned before, in an urban setting, that is nowhere enough when you add in transportation, cell phones, credit card purchases, and payments, purchase a computer, internet access, and all the other things required to live today, including housing, child care, and food. According to a 2018 British Broadcasting company report, 75% of Americans are barely able to afford a place to live or food to eat. I saw this all the time in my IRS work. People were struggling to make ends meet. Parents were working three jobs but never had enough money. In high-cost cities such as San Francisco, even a family of four earning $117,400 is considered to be in "near poverty." Yet the *Tax Payer Advocate Service* (TAS) report showed that hundreds of thousands of wealthy taxpayers had been allowed to skip filing taxes altogether. In 2015, the IRS had lost so many collection employees that it could not work most of its cases. However, because of Covid-19, over 2 million non-filer investigations are scheduled to be restarted if Congress passes the funding.

And for those who can remember, once upon a time, in the '50s, a family could own a home, a car, and send the kids to college, all on one income. Then Congress cut taxes on the rich, and the middle class died.

Why Doesn't the IRS Go After the *Rich People*?

"The big man plays, while the little man pays."

—**Johnny Paycheck song**

The tax system does a very poor job of taxing the rich and a great job taxing the working poor. During the time of Covid-19, the *Rich People* have gotten much richer. The 630 *billionaires* in the United States have gotten $931 billion richer. That is a fact. You could never get that much money just by being a wage earner—a wage slave, because the tax laws are designed and handwritten for *Rich People, Big Businesses, and Corporations*, not you.

This fact alone should be the beginning of massive tax reform, but in reality, the tax system is being used as a tool for social conditioning and control. Keeping wages low and introducing new tax laws that benefit the rich make rising out of poverty almost impossible.

Charles O. Rossotti, a former IRS Commissioner Natasha Sarin, a University of Pennsylvania Professor; and Lawrence Summers, a former Treasury Secretary have projected in their report—(see Chapter 17) that returning the IRS to funding levels of the past or adding 6% or more to the yearly budget (about $80 billion total over ten years) **would increase enforcement spending and strategies which would generate $1.2-$1.4 trillion more in taxes, primarily from the *Rich People for the benefit of the United States*.**

CHAPTER 5

HOW TO FIGHT THE IRS —KNOWLEDGE IS POWER

Knowing that one day your unpaid taxes will go away completely will give you hope and peace of mind. This book aims to educate you on tax laws and methods used to work collection cases by the IRS. Let me tell you; it does not matter if the tax balances are ever paid off.

Let's Start with the Audit

Are you worried about being audited? Three years after the April 15 filing due date, you will not be audited if you have timely filed your tax returns. On April 15, 2021, you will not need to worry about your 2017 tax return being audited. You can also stop worrying about whatever you put on the returns for 2016, 2015, 2014, 2013, 2012, 2011, and 2010. In 2022 you won't need to worry about your 2018 taxes being audited. For this assessment statute to begin, you have to file your tax returns timely. However, if you haven't filled or improperly calculated your taxes for 2018, you should worry.

Collection

Your tax balance is legally "written off" after ten years. Ten years from the date that the IRS has processed your tax return and shows that you have a legally assessed tax, your income taxes and business taxes will expire and go away forever. The IRS never tells you this. This lack of transparency hurts the lower and middle classes the most. Finding out what your *Collection Statue of Expirations Date* (CSED) is made as difficult as possible for taxpayers (40% of taxpayers who try to get their personal tax information fail). This is called the **Collection Statute of Expirations Date.** (CSED) You need to know what this date is.

Here's How to Find the Date

Using the IRS *Transcript Delivery System* (TDS), order the online selection *Get Transcript* then select *Account Transcript*. Next, look for *Transaction Code TC 150* (tax assessed), *TC 290* (additional tax adjustment assessment), or *TC 300* (audit-additional tax or deficiency by examination division.) That date is the legal date that the tax was assessed. It is ten years from that date when the tax assessment expires, and you will no longer owe the tax balance. Also, any *Notice of Federal Tax Liens* will expire and can be removed for the year you're assessed. An example would be: you owed the IRS $50,000 in 2011; your tax balance will expire in 2021, and you will owe nothing even if there is a balance remaining.

See the end of this chapter for all Examples Exhibit Forms

For many people establishing an account on the IRS computer is not as easy as it sounds. Finding your *Collection Statue of Expirations Date* is hard, but it is worth the time it takes to do so. Holding a stack of your tax transcripts with all your dates will bring you peace of mind seeing that magical date published when your taxes go away forever!

For those of you who struggle with accessing this information, you may email me at Richard@RMSTaxconsulting.com, and for a fee, I will get your limited power of attorney and then go into the IRS computer and pull your transcripts and advise you on the *Collection Statue of Expirations Date*. My review will tell you:

- Total tax assessment, penalty, interest, and accrual amounts for each year (so you know how much you owe).

- *Collection Statue of Expirations Date* (CSED) calculations for each year requested.
- Tolling events (if any) and the days your CSED has been extended. (Tolling means an event has occurred which extends the statute of collections, such as an appeal or offer in compromise.
- All IRS notices sent/received for each year.
- IRS account activity by year.

It is essential to determine how long the delinquent tax will be due and what can be done about the delinquent tax in the meantime. Note that: *if a case is an installment agreement or has been identified as Currently Not Collectible, this does not extend the Collection Statue of Expirations Date.*

Here is the bad news that the IRS doesn't tell you. The following events do extend the *Collection Statue of Expirations Date*:

- Filing an *Offer in Compromise*—if it is rejected.
- Filing Bankruptcy—if the bankruptcy is dismissed, not discharged.
- Going to Tax Court—you can represent yourself (Pro Se).
- Going to Appeals, Filing a Collection Due Process Appeal.
- You are out of the USA for more than six months.
- The IRS decides that it would be in the government's best interests to extend the CSED based upon case circumstances.
- If the taxpayer owes the IRS and has committed what the IRS regards as a tax crime, or the taxpayer is conspiring to evade taxes, the IRS can file suit to extend the collection statute twenty years or more into the future with a tax judgment in federal court. However, this is extremely rare.

Here's an odd factoid. Al Capone's assets are still under a *Collection Statue of Expirations Date* into perpetuity even though he is dead.

If you are looking at a tax transcript, there can be more than one CSED. For example, if you filed your 2020 return and it is assessed on April 15, 2021, then the IRS's ability to collect on that debt expires on April 15, 2031. It is important to know that each period or each year has its *Collection Statue of Expirations Date*. Generally, 2018 taxes filed by 4-15-2019 will expire 4-15-2029. 2019 filed 4-15-2020 will expire 4-15-2030.

In this example of April 15, 2031, if the taxpayer had been audited on June 27, 2022, then the new CSED for the increased tax amount would be June 27, 2032.

If you are looking at a Notice of Federal Tax Lien, this is the assessment date shown in Column (d) Date of Assessment. The tax expires on that day, but the IRS has 30 days to refile it. So, the last day for refiling is shown in Column (e).

If you owe a reasonable amount of money (the price of a new car) and think that you can pay it off in the next seven years, you don't need this. If you have financial difficulties and think they will worsen, you need your CSED and all the relevant information you can get.

On some newer balance due letters (CP14 and others), there is a Q.R. scan code that you can take a picture of on your smartphone, which will connect you to the IRS computer system. It should take only 15 minutes to sign up to get access, but you need all of your present and past tax information to validate who you are. For any cases with a balance due for the years 2010 to 2014, you do need a *Collection Status Expiration Date* for accurate planning of your options. You may be closer than you think to having the IRS write off your tax balance.

Remember, the IRS will not share your CSED with you unless you ask them, and it is hard to get anyone to talk to. Why is this? They don't answer the phone because they are too few employees. Budget cuts to the IRS hurt everyone. The IRS might not calculate the CSED correctly, and unchallenged that adds years to your IRS drama. When the CSED expires, the IRS does not tell you that, it just enters a code TC 608 on your transcript and writes off the balance due. It never tells you.

You might continue paying your tax balance when you don't need to. Sometimes taxpayers continue making installment agreement payments long after the CSED has expired. Though one day, you may get a refund check for the overpaid amounts. This forces you to make a phone call to the agency. Hopefully, they will answer and clear up the issue.

Your CSED date is important to know, and it will guide you in what you should do financially and tax-wise in the remaining time you owe the IRS. Always continue to file and pay current taxes and then wait and see what the IRS does—if anything.

That is why knowledge is power and will bring you peace of mind. Keep reading!

EXHIBITS 1–10

Exhibits 1-10

Exhibit #1: *Notice of Federal Tax Lien*

Form 668 (Y)(c)
(Rev. February 2004)

Department of the Treasury - Internal Revenue Service
Notice of Federal Tax Lien

Area:

Serial Number

For Optional Use by Recording Office

As provided by section 6321, 6322, and 6323 of the Internal Revenue Code, we are giving a notice that taxes (including interest and penalties) have been assessed against the following-named taxpayer. We have made a demand for payment of this liability, but it remains unpaid. Therefore, there is a lien in favor of the United States on all property and rights to property belonging to this taxpayer for the amount of these taxes, and additional penalties, interest, and costs that may accrue.

Name of Taxpayer

Residence

IMPORTANT RELEASE INFORMATION: For each assessment listed below, unless notice of the lien is refiled by the date given in column (e), this notice shall, on the day following such date, operation as a certificate of release as defined in IRC 6325(a).

Kind of Tax (a)	Tax Period Ending (b)	Identifying Number (c)	Date of Assessment (d)	Last Day for Refiling (e)	Unpaid Balance of Assessment (f)

Place of Filing

Total $

This notice was prepared and signed at _____, on this,

the _____ day of _____, ____.

Signature

Title

NOTE: Certificate of officer authorized by law to take acknowledgment is not essential to the validity of Notice of Federal Tax lien
Rev. Rul. 71-466, 1971 - 2 C.B. 4096

Part 1 - Kept By Recording Office

Form 668 (Y) (c) (Rev. 2-2004)
CAT. NO 60025X

47

Exhibit #2: *IRS Transcript Type*

Transcript Types and Ways to Order Them

Ways to Get Transcripts

You may register to use Get Transcript Online to view, print, or download all transcript types listed below.

If you're unable to register or you prefer not to use Get Transcript Online, you may order a **tax return transcript** and/or a **tax account transcript** using Get Transcript by Main or call 800-908-9946. Please **allow 5 to 10 clandar days for delivery.**

You may also request any transcript type listed below by faxing/mailing Form 4506-T, Request for Transcript of Tax Return as instructed on the form.

Transcript Types

We offer the following transcript types at no charge to you:

- **Tax Return Transcript**—shows most line items including your **adjusted gross income (AGI)** from your original Form 1040-series tax return as filed, along with any forms and schedules. It doesn't show changes made after you filed your original return. This transcript is only available for the current tax year and returns processed during the prior three years. A tax return transcript usually meets the needs of lending institutions offering mortgages and student loans. **Note:** the secondary spouse on a joint return must use Get Transcript Online or Form 4506-T to request this transcript type. When using Get Transcript by Mail or phone, the primary taxpayer on the return must make the request.

- **Tax Account Transcript**—shows basic data such as return type, marital status, adjusted gross income, taxable income and all payment types. It also shows changes made after you filed your original return. This transcript is available for the current tax year and up to 10 prior years using Get Transcript Online or Form 4506-T. When using Get Transcript by Mail or phone, you're limited to the current tax year and returns processed during the prior three years. Note: If you made estimated tax payments and/or applied an overpayment from a prior year return, you can request this transcript type a few weeks after the beginning of the calendar year to confirm your payments prior to filing your tax return.

- **Record of Account Transcript**—combines the tax return and tax account transcripts above into one complete transcript. This transcript is available for the current tax year and returns processed during the prior three years using Get Transcript Online or Form 4506-T.

- **Wage and Income Transcript**—shows data from information returns we receive such as Forms W-2, 1099, 1098 and Form 5498, IRA Contribution Information. Current tax year information may not be complete until July. This transcript is available for up to 10 prior years using Get Transcript Online or Form 4506-T.

- **Verification of Non-filing Letter**—provides proof that the IRS has no record of a filed Form 1040-series tax return for the year you requested. It doesn't indicate whether you were required to file a return for that year. This letter is available after June 15 for the current tax year or anytime for the prior three tax years using Get Transcript Online or Form 4506-T. You must use Form 4506-T if you need a letter for tax years older than the prior three years.

Note: A transcript can show return and/or account data. It also can show changes or transactions made after you filed your original return. Transaction codes consist of three digits. They are used to identify a transaction being processed and to maintain a history of actions posted to a taxpayer's account. For further information regarding transaction codes, please see Document 11734 - Transaction Code Pocket Guide PDF.

Note: A transcript isn't a photocopy of your return. If you need a copy of your original return, complete and mail Form 4506, Request for Copy of Tax Return, along with the applicable fee.

Refer to Get Transcript frequently asked questions for more information.

Exhibit #3: *Get Your Tax Record*

Welcome to Get Transcript

What's New?

There is a new transcript format that better protects your data. This new format partially masks your personally identifiable information. Financial data will remain fully visible to allow for tax preparation, tax representation or income verification. Learn more at About the New Tax Transcript and the Customer File Number.

Caution: The Get Transcript Service is for individual taxpayers to retrieve their own transcripts for their own purposes. Use by any other entities is prohibited.

You can get various Form 1040-series transcript types online or by mail. If you need your prior year **Adjusted Gross Income (AGI)** to e-file, choose the ***tax return transcript*** type when making your request. To find out how much you owe or to verify your payment history, you can view your tax account.

The method you used to file your tax return, e-file or paper, and whether you had a balance due, affects your current year transcript availability. **Note:** If you need a photocopy of your return, you must use Form 4506.

Request Online

What You Need

To register and use this service, you need:

- your SSN, date of birth, filing status and mailing address from latest tax return, access to your email account,

- your personal account number from a credit card, mortgage, home equity loan, home equity line of credit or car loan, and

- a mobile phone linked to your name (for faster registration) or ability to receive an activation code by mail.

What You Get

- All transcript types are available online
- View, print or download your transcript
- Username and password to return later

Request by Mail

What You Need

- To use this service, you need your:
- SSN or Individual Tax Identification Number (ITIN),
- date of birth, and
- mailing address from your latest tax return

What You Get

- Return or Account transcript types delivered by mail
- Transcripts arrive in 5 to 10 calendar days at the address we have on file for you

Exhibit #4: *Exhibit Sign Up*

Sign Up

Don't have an account? Create one now.

CREATE ACCOUNT >

Log In

Already have a username? Welcome back!

Username

LOG IN >

Forgot Username

Warning: By accessing and using this government computer system, you are consenting to system monitoring, interception, recording, reading, copying or capturing by authorized personnel of all activities, including detection and prevention of any unauthorized use of this system. The system you are accessing contains confidential tax information and is designed exclusively for use by authorized persons to interact with the IRS and retrieve confidential tax information using only their own account. Any other use of this system that is inconsistent with the intended purposes of the system is an unauthorized use of the system and strictly prohibited.

Do not create or access an account in this system for anyone other than yourself. You may not use another person's information to create or access an account on behalf of and in the name of that person, even if that person provided their information to you to create or access an account for them or even if that person consented to your use of their information to create or access the account.

Unauthorized use of this system is prohibited and subject to criminal and civil penalties, including, but not limited to, penalties applicable to knowingly or intentionally accessing a computer without authorization or exceeding authorized access under 18 USC. 1030.

Exhibits 1-10

Exhibit #5: *You Will Need to Register*

You will need to register in order to use this service

Registration is:

Fast: Signing up only takes about 15 minutes.

Secure: Only you will have access to your tax information.

Convenient: You will only need to verify your identity once.

Free: There is no charge to sign up (Message and data rates may apply to send a security code to your mobile phone).

Before we get started, we're going to ask you some simple questions to make sure you have everything you need.

53

Exhibit #6: *You Will Need Some Information About Yourself to Register*

You will need some information about yourself to register

Please have the following information and materials to complete registration

- Full Name
- Email
- Birthdate
- Social Security Number (SSN) or Individual Tax Identification Number (ITIN)
- Tax filing status
- Current address
- Do you have this information available?

Do you have this information available?

Exhibit #7: *You Will Need a Financial Account to Register*

You will need a financial account to register

To verify your identity, we will need a number from ONE of your financial accounts. We can use any of the following:

- Last 8 digits of Visa, Mastercard, or Discover credit card OR
- Student loan OR
- Mortgage or home equity loan OR
- Home equity line of credit OR
- Auto loan

You will only need to provide the loan account number or a few digits from a credit card number. We only use this information to verify your identity. **You will not be charged any money and are not sharing any account balances or other financial information with us.**

We can't verify debit cards, corporate cards, American Express, Barclays, or some cards issued by banks in US territories. Additionally, we can't verify student loans issued by Nelnet.

A soft inquiry will show up on your credit report to let you know that the IRS accessed your credit report information. This will not increase or decrease your credit score and lenders will not be able to see this.

Do you have this financial information available? (If you don't have the account information on hand, you should answer 'No'.)

Exhibit #8: *You Need a Phone Number or Verified Address*

You need a phone number or verified address

We'll need one more way to verify your identity. The easiest way is to send a code to your phone by text message (SMS). Your phone must be a US-based mobile phone number associated with your name.

You can also complete identity verification by receiving a letter in the mail. If you choose this method, you'll either need a US-based phone number OR an iPhone, iPad, or Android device to complete registration.

CONTINUE >

Exhibit #9: *Let's Get Started!*

You will need a financial account to register

To verify your identity, we will need a number from ONE of your financial accounts. We can use any of the following:

- Last 8 digits of Visa, Mastercard, or Discover credit card OR
- Student loan OR
- Mortgage or home equity loan OR
- Home equity line of credit OR
- Auto loan

You will only need to provide the loan account number or a few digits from a credit card number. We only use this information to verify your identity. **You will not be charged any money and are not sharing any account balances or other financial information with us.**

We can't verify debit cards, corporate cards, American Express, Barclays, or some cards issued by banks in US territories. Additionally, we can't verify student loans issued by Nelnet.

A soft inquiry will show up on your credit report to let you know that the IRS accessed your credit report information. This will not increase or decrease your credit score and lenders will not be able to see this.

Do you have this financial information available? (If you don't have the account information on hand, you should answer 'No'.)

> **Exhibit #10:** *View Your Account Information*

Your Account Information

Online Account is an online system that allows you to securely access your individual account information.

[Create or view your account]

If you have questions about how to create an account, see Secure Access: How to Register for Certain Online Self-Help Tools.

You can view:

- The total amount you owe, including balance details by year
- Your payment history and any scheduled or pending payments
- Key information from your most recent tax return
- Payment plan details, if you have one
- Digital copies of select notices from the IRS
- Your Economic Impact Payments, if any
- Your address on file
- Authorization requests from tax professionals

You can also:

- Make a payment online
- See payment plan options and request a plan via Online Payment Agreement
- Access your tax records via Get Transcript
- Approve or reject authorization requests from tax professionals

Please note:

- Your balance will update no more than once every 24 hours, usually overnight.
- Check or money order payments may take up to 3 weeks to appear in your account.

For additional help, see our Frequently Asked Questions About Online Account.

Hours of availability

- Monday 6 a.m. to Saturday 9 p.m. ET
- Sunday: 10 a.m. to midnight ET (Occasionally down additional hours for maintenance)

Accessibility

There are compatibility issues with some assistive technologies. Refer to the accessibility guide for help if you use a screen reader, screen magnifier or voice command software.

Notice: iOS 11, macOS 10.12, and macOS 10.13 VoiceOver users may experience difficulties when accessing this application. If this impacts you, please refer to the "Other ways to find your account information" section.

Other ways to find your account information

- You can request an Account Transcript. Please note that each Account Transcript only covers a single tax year, and may not show the most recent penalties, interest, changes or pending actions.
- If you're a business, or an individual who filed a form other than 1040, you can obtain a transcript by submitting Form 4506-T, Request for Transcript of Tax Return.
- Find more assistance.

CHAPTER 6
DO I NEED A TAX PROFESSIONAL TO GET THE BEST DEAL?

Do you need a tax professional to help you get the best deal from the IRS? The IRS is so convoluted, and each case has different aspects to it. So, the answer would be "Yes," "No," and "Maybe." If you face irregular income, loss of income or employment, or health or other financial issues, then yes, a tax professional may be able to help you resolve your tax case.

No, if you owe under $10,000 and are able to make payments. Maybe if you feel that you cannot pay now or in the future or you have other major issues such as a change in house location, chronic illness, or other problems.

Many people claim to be able to help you with your IRS problems. Some are called tax resolution professionals, and some are tax preparers. If you owe money to IRS, you may need a Tax Resolution Professional or Enrolled Agent.

What are Enrolled Agents?

An Enrolled Agent is a person who has proven proficiency in federal tax planning, individual and business tax return preparation, and representation. They must complete 72 hours of continuing education every three years. Enrolled Agents can do business in all 50 states.

Some Enrolled Agents are retired or former IRS employees with at least five years' experience who automatically qualify for Enrolled Agent status because of their knowledge, experience, and education.

Retired *IRS Revenue Officers and IRS Revenue Agents* can be great advocates for collection and appeals, audit, and *Offer in Compromise* cases. They will be your advocate, and they have a fiduciary responsibility to take care of you in a competent professional manner. They know the tax law and IRS procedures and how the IRS will review or decide your case. They know the latest deals that the IRS is offering.

Sometimes the Enrolled Agent will discover that you have done things in your taxes that might expose you to an IRS Criminal Investigation. They can still represent you. See the attorney-client privilege below.

I became an Enrolled Agent. When I retired because I wanted to help people in trouble with the IRS. One of the last cases that I worked at the IRS involved a taxpayer (let's call him Jim) owed the IRS $17,000. Jim had paid $7,000 to a law firm to represent him before the IRS. That law firm then filed for bankruptcy. So, I was knocking on Jim's door at 8 AM. When Jim saw me and my IRS credentials, he told me that he had an attorney and did not want to talk to me. He told me that he was afraid of the IRS. I explained to Jim that the law firm had gone bankrupt but that I could offer him an installment agreement with easy payment terms.

The whole process took 20 minutes. The more I thought about Jim's case, the more outraged I got at what that law firm had done to him. I wondered how many other people had been ripped off like that. Surprisingly, I never knew before how much all tax professionals charged their clients. That was a real eye-opener to me, which lead to my new career in tax resolution as an Enrolled Agent.

Attorney-Client-Enrolled Agent Privilege

Do you know what attorney-client privilege is? It means that anything you tell the attorney, they can never repeat that information to another person, even if they are under a summons or subpoena. Your private financial business stays just between the two of you.

A Certified Public Accountant (CPA) or Enrolled Agent has limited confidentiality protection. Of course, they must not go about sharing your business; they must keep all of your communications private and confidential. But if they are summoned or subpoenaed, they have to tell the IRS everything that you told them.

Some clients hire a tax attorney, and then the tax attorney hires the CPA and the Enrolled Agent as needed to work your case. Here, the attorney-client privilege covers the Attorney, the CPA, and the Enrolled Agent. This is because of a case called the *United States v. Kovel*, 296 F.2d 918 (2d Cir. 1961). Currently, I have an attorney on retainer connected to my firm who does this for my clients. Thus, the attorney-client privilege extends to me. For you readers, this scenario of attorney and confidentiality should be explored before you hire a tax professional.

Certified Public Accountants (CPAs)

CPAs offer a range of services from bookkeeping to tax planning, tax preparation, and financial planning and bring an unmatched level of knowledge, experience, and education to the tax planning and preparation process. Many CPAs specialize in certain types of businesses, such as partnerships or corporate tax work. Most have a mix of business and personal tax clients.

A CPA can make a tax plan for you that will save you tax money and provide for retirement planning long into the future. A CPA is an excellent choice for an audit case.

The best CPA will interview you about your financial situation, family situation, and life goals and listen to you and respond to your questions. They will also be available for year-end tax planning from October to December.

However, you should know CPAs may be very qualified to represent you in an audit or appeals situation but usually have no idea what to do in a collection or criminal case.

Never Hire These Tax Firms

Let's start with the tax professionals that abuse the taxpaying public with false and misleading ads promising that they will get

Offers-in-Compromise and tax settlements for pennies on the dollar. Their business practices are unethical. Often what they promise is untrue and illegal.

These firms sell hope—like the snake oil salesman of the 1800s. This false belief generates income that snowballs into more ads selling promises. They sell the notion that by hiring them, you will be able to get the IRS off your back for good—that you will be able to settle your tax debt with the IRS for pennies on the dollar. It is a nice dream. It is my experience that they are mostly unable to deliver on their promises.

I advocate avoiding the big box tax resolution firms. These are the ones you see advertising all the time on the media. Their promises could charge you up to ten times what a local tax professional could charge.

In my career, I have had four clients who hired these villains, and each owed under $100,000 to the IRS. My clients had no unusual circumstances. They each paid $20,000 for tax representation to the big box resolution firm. You ask, "Is $20,000 too much?" Absolutely! Generally, the fees will range from $1000 to $2500 unless there are complications, and it might run $5,000.

All tax professionals should explain upfront exactly what they will do and approximately what it will cost them to do. They should tell you that representing you in an audit will take approximately so many hours and disclose their rate per hour. If going to the Office of Appeals on your case is an option, they should give you a separate quote for how much that is expected to cost.

I practice in Tucson, Arizona, where Enrolled Agents charge $100-$250 an hour, CPA's $250-$350 an hour, and tax attorneys $350 and up. They can all save you money. Sometime, I just consult with clients about their case on a limited basis to give them information regarding what they should do, and then they are able to go forward themselves and save money.

I believe in being upfront with all expected charges and expenses. This is called transparency. Unfortunately, far too many tax preparers and tax resolution specialists resist consumers' preference to "price shop." It is very hard for consumers to compare prices. This limits competition and produces secrecy and fear in consumers, and costs consumers more money all the way around.

Some tax professionals will give you a flat rate quote, and then if you want to go to higher levels like Appeals or Tax Court, they will offer you a separate price quote.

Tax professionals use an engagement letter that tells you what they will do, and then you review and sign it. That is your contract with them. In most businesses like mine, when you owe the taxes to IRS, you pay the tax professional the fee for services upfront.

When you talk to your tax professional and feel comfortable, you will give them your limited power of attorney power for tax matters so they can research your case directly on the IRS computer. When you do this, the IRS cannot call you or contact you; the IRS has to contact your tax representative. The only time you would be required to speak to the IRS is if you receive a summons to appear and provide records and testimony. You can have your representative by your side.

Helpful Hints When Choosing a Return Preparer

- Avoid tax preparers that are in temporary locations. They pop up for tax season and then close shop after tax season. If they can't afford to have a decent office that is open year-round and provide tax work and bookkeeping, walk on by.

- If a tax preparer wants to meet you at Starbucks or in the parking lot and works out of the trunk of his car or at your kitchen table, avoid them.

- If the tax preparer does not have a PTIN (Preparer Tax Identification Number), a number required by the IRS for all people who prepare and file tax returns, then avoid them.

- The IRS issued a report that identified 19,496 tax preparers with PTINs who were non-compliant with filing and paying their tax obligations. (These preparers had $367 million in taxes due as of January 26, 2015. Also, 3,055 preparers failed to file tax returns for one or more years, and eight tax return preparers failed to file required returns for five years.)

- If the tax preparer refuses to sign the tax return or put their business name or PTIN on your tax return, then you should not sign it either.

- Be cautious of tax preparers who claim that they can get you larger tax refunds than other tax preparers.

- Avoid preparers who base their fee on a percentage of the refund. Use a reputable tax preparer who signs the return and gives you a copy.

- Consider if the tax preparer will be around after the tax season to answer questions, handle a tax audit for you, or explain what happened if you do not receive a tax refund.

- If you are making a "direct deposit" of your refund, it should be deposited directly into your bank account, not the tax preparer's account. Some refunds can come as a Debit Card. Debit cards should come to your home address, not the tax preparer's address. Tax returns should have your home address, not the tax preparers.

- Ask if the tax preparer is affiliated with a professional organization that provides its members with continuing education and resources and holds them to a code of conduct and ethics. They should be happy to tell you.

- Never sign a blank return or sign the *E-Filing Authorization* (*Form 8879*) until you have reviewed the return and gotten a copy of it. This could lead to potential fraud by the tax preparer.

Can You Prepare Your Own Tax Return?

You need the right person to do your tax return. After the Trump Tax Cuts Bill of 2017, tax returns are much easier to fill out yourself. Because of the changes in the law, most people (66%) cannot itemize deductions anymore. So, your medical bills, state income taxes, mortgage interest, donations to charities have probably been figured into your tax status, and you don't need to itemize them to get a lower tax rate. It is more likely you can do your return yourself if you only have a W-2 wage income or a small business, even if you claim the *Earned Income Tax Credit*. If you follow the tax software's instructions, then you should be able to prepare an acceptable tax return. However, many people are so terrified of the IRS and fearful of making an error, they have more peace of mind finding a tax preparer who charges them a reasonable price.

In 2019, more than 34.5 million people paid for tax software even though they qualified for *Free File* software from the same provider. For example, you can get Turbo-Tax for free if you earned under $72,000.

If you have more complicated issues such as a Covid-19 related illness, loss or job or business, death in the family, trust, inheritance, etc., I suggest you consult an Enrolled Agent.

If your income is over $72,000, the **irs.gov/freefile** and **Free File Alliance (freefilealliance.org)** offers no-cost tax prep software if your total income, minus certain amounts as retirement plan contributions, is $72,000 or less. Yet, "free" can cost you if special circumstances arise as you are paying your taxes. You never know.

The IRS's new policy is to refer taxpayers to the IRS website, where they are "shopped-out" to private organizations, some of whom receive money from the IRS to help taxpayers. The IRS does not want to see or hear from the taxpayers it is sending letters to.

Services For Americans

One program is called the *Volunteer Income Tax Assistance (VITA)* program. This program offers free tax help to people who generally make $54,000 or less, persons with disabilities, the elderly, and limited English-speaking taxpayers who need assistance in preparing their tax returns. IRS-certified volunteers provide free essential income tax return preparation with electronic filing to qualified individuals in the following organizations.

Low-Income Taxpayer Clinics (LITCs) represent low-income individuals in disputes with the Internal Revenue Service, including audits, appeals, collection matters, and federal tax litigation. LITCs provide education about taxpayer rights and responsibilities for low-income taxpayers and taxpayers who speak English as a second language (ESL).

The *IRS Tax Counseling for the Elderly (TCE)* program offers free tax help for all taxpayers, particularly those 60 years of age or older, specializing in questions about pensions and retirement-related issues unique to seniors. The IRS-certified volunteers who provide tax counseling are often retired individuals associated with non-profit organizations that receive grants from the IRS.

The *AARP* (the American Association of Retired Persons) operates most **TCE** sites, and you can call 1-888-227-7669 to find a location near you.

Big Name Tax Preparers

Going with big-name tax preparers like H&R Block, Liberty Tax, etc., is the answer for some people. They have many employees who can be very knowledgeable, but their services cost a lot of money. Last year, H& R Block, the largest independent tax preparation company with 11,000 offices, had $3 billion in revenues from people just like you. Jackson Hewitt is a company that has 5,800 local offices as well as online software. Some of its stores are located in Walmart's and mall locations.

These corporate companies offer loans on your tax refund. These are called *refund anticipation loans* and come with high fees and interest charges. It's like the Pay Day Loan Scam. They are a big rip-off! Don't do this. I recommend that you adjust your income tax withholding to get more back in each paycheck and a smaller refund at the end of the year. Ask your employer to file a *Form W-4, Employees Withholding Allowance Certificate* to increase your paycheck.

Unenrolled Preparers—Another Scam

Some preparers are called unenrolled preparers. They cannot talk to the IRS about your return; they have little or no tax law education and are not regulated or monitored by anyone, especially not the IRS. Usually, they set up a lucrative practice in a storefront and then stay one or two tax seasons and have been known to do outrageous things with tax returns that include fraudulent returns and even forging a client's signature and stealing their refunds. They then close the business when the IRS starts to match up all the information on the returns with information from other sources.

A fresh approach from Darren Hillot, IRS Deputy Commissioner was his office message on November 20, 2020:

> If you're struggling with your tax bill, reach out to us. Don't be intimidated. Our people can help you walk through it. And if you need the services of a tax professional, that's a great option as well. But please take a few minutes to do some research first. Make sure you're getting a reputable representative, and not some fly-by-night outfit on late-night television or the radio that charges fees for things the IRS does for free—or at a minimal cost. We appreciate the support of tax professionals and other partners in getting the word out—I know they're just as committed as we are to helping those in need.

This is a refreshingly candid comment from a leader in the IRS, but since the IRS acknowledges that it only answers 22% of all phone calls received. So, it is a hollow comment.

CHAPTER 7
AUDITS ARE FOR EVERYONE, EVEN CRIMINALS!

In 2021 the IRS audit rates have been the lowest that they have been since the soldiers went away to fight World War II. This is because the most experienced *IRS Auditors* and *Revenue Agents* have retired, and very few have been hired to replace them. Audits can be financially messy and revealing. They always upset *Rich People, Big Businesses, and Corporations* who reach out to the members of Congress with large campaign donations. This is how the tax laws are changed and crafted to meet their demands and needs, not the needs of the general public.

In 2011, 80% of people who earned more than $1 million were audited, and today it is only about 2% of the people who earned more than $1 million who are audited.

Remember, budget cuts have emasculated the agency, dropping the audit rate every year since 2005.

IRS Commissioner Charles Rettig admits to this. He claims that this is cheaper and faster to audit a poor person than a rich one. This would be the wage earner of a family making under $40,000 per year. Often poor people are socially mobile and change jobs more frequently due to financial hardship. Some are even homeless. When their return was filed, they may have listed their old address on their return, so they don't even get the IRS letters, and those that do are afraid to respond to the IRS out of fear of financial repercussions.

In general, 42 % fewer audits were conducted between 2010 and 2017, according to a *ProPublica* report. IRS audits for people earning over $1 million a year plunged 81% from 2011 to 2019. The IRS opened audits on only 0.03 of returns reporting income of $10 million or more in 2018.

Audit rates for those people making $10 million or more annually have fallen by 80%. But the number of audits on low-income *Earned Income Tax Credit* (EITC) cases has risen by 50%. Nine out of 10 audits result in new tax balances.

According to a report by the Treasury Inspector General for Tax Administration (TIGTA) 09-13-2020, due to lack of resources, the IRS failed to audit more than 897,000 rich taxpayers who skipped out on filing and paying tax returns over a three-year period-and these individuals owe nearly $46 billion in taxes.

2019 brought the lowest tax rates in the last sixty years. Corporate audits with income over $20 billion used to be audited every year; now, only 50% of them are audited.

In 2010 the IRS collected $28 billion from audits adjusted for inflation. In 2019 it collected only $11 billion, a drop of 61%. I think that that is a horrifying fact. It is criminal for Congress to have so savagely destroyed the IRS. Again, it is the best of times to not file or pay your taxes and the worst of times for the IRS and other taxpayers. This needs to stop!

Again, this is good for those people who are filing tax returns wherein they or their accountant have taken what is called "aggressive tax positions." That means that they are trying to push the limits of the law. Increasingly, tax professionals are working more and more to help clients with audits during this window of opportunity.

The number of IRS audit agents has dropped to the lowest level since the 1950s, while the USA's population has more than doubled from the 1950s to 2021. Did you know that there were 13,879 *Revenue Agents* in 2010? In 2020, the number was 8,234 *Revenue Agents*, with additional agents retiring every day. This brings the IRS staff down 41% in total agents in the past ten years!

Let's get down to some definitions. The IRS Service Center conducts Tax Adjustments. IRS Tax Audits are conducted by:

- *Revenue Agents* (RA) are the most highly trained and experienced auditors with substantial accounting skills and investigative techniques—they are attorneys, CPAs, economists, and IRS engineers who can audit complex tax returns and secure payment of taxes owed.
- *Tax Examiners* (TEs) and *Tax Compliance Officers* (TCO) conduct audits and reviews less complex tax law issues.

Tax Adjustments—What does the IRS Do?

The IRS reviews all income tax returns. When something on your return looks different from other tax returns, it triggers a second look by the IRS. They will send you a tax adjustment letter (CP2000) stating that you owe additional taxes. The letter states what your new tax amount will be. They want you to pay the amount shown in the letter.

This is not an audit; it is just the IRS matching up information reported to it. For example, you might receive a 1099 and forget to list the income on your tax return. The IRS does not want you in their office, and they certainly don't want you to call them. The IRS does not care if you did it on purpose or if you forgot. They want you to pay the amount shown in the letter. The average amount owed on the *CP2000* notice in 2019 was $1,893.

The IRS compares what you put on your tax return to what others have reported that they paid to you in *W-2 Forms* and *Form 1099* income. They check to see if you are under-reporting income. The IRS will also add up your numbers and check for mathematical errors or to see if you calculated deductions or credits on your return correctly. Even though these tax adjustment letters are scary to receive in the mail, you should check your tax records and reply in writing. Math error notices just look like bills; they don't tell you why you owe them money, just tell you to pay it now! You probably don't need a tax professional to help you respond.

Mail Audits

76% of all audits are mail audits. In this case, the IRS sends you a letter requesting information and proof of something you put on your tax return (two to three years prior). This "letter" looks like a bill. For example, Jim gets a letter for 2018 taxes asking for proof of dependents. You can see that this limits the audit scope, and Jim doesn't have to talk to an IRS agent. This is the least painful type of audit because it is usually only on one to three issues. Since the mail audits always cover past years' taxes, you either have the proof the IRS wants or not.

Sadly, two-thirds of the people who are audited by mail never protest the IRS judgment. Why? Many people are afraid to challenge the IRS and choose to send a check to pay the proposed adjusted amount the IRS claims they owe. When you do not respond, the audit becomes fact, and you owe the new tax plus penalties and interest.

Shockingly, a Treasurer Inspector General tax audit determined that 20% of all IRS audits and adjustments are in error. Taxpayers could have successfully challenged their mail audit if only they had known that they had the right to challenge the audit.

This affects the low-income population the most because they may not have access to tax professionals and may not understand the information that the IRS is questioning. How do you respond and say that you don't agree with the proposed audit amounts? The IRS audit letters are confusing and threatening. It is hard to know your audit rights when you are struggling all by yourself. Also, there is no actual form to be used to protest the audit.

Office Audits

Because of Covid-19, since April 2020, there have been no in-person audits in IRS buildings, and they are not expected to start again until Spring 2022. The IRS is conducting audits by telephone and mail instead. As was mentioned before, many people write a check to the IRS because they are scared and pay what is stated in the IRS letter before closely examining the information presented.

If the IRS audits you and comes up with a higher tax amount

plus penalties and interest, you have a tax adjustment. Or the IRS can accept your return as filed, and that is called a "no-change audit." Additionally, 26,000 people in 2019 were audited, resulting in those taxpayers receiving a refund. The refunds issued were $78.9 billion that year due to poor case selection criteria.

There were 771,795 audits in 2019, but many of the audits might have had wrong information, and only 20,000 people challenged the tax adjustment (2.6%). With the 20% error rate, this illustrates the way the IRS uses fear to harm people.

Another specific type of audit is for small businesses that the IRS might consider to be hobbies and thus will not allow any business expenses. Jim has a woodworking shop and spent his mother's inheritance on machinery. Here's an example. Jim makes bird houses to sell to friends and neighbors. He claimed the machinery on his tax return. But the IRS said Jim has a hobby, and a tax adjustment disallowed all of his purchases and expenses, now the tax plus penalties and interest has ruined his life.

Internal Revenue Auditors and Agents work cases that are complicated and may contain multiple issues. No matter how clean your records are, I always tell my clients to hire a tax professional, either an Enrolled Agent or a CPA, and that they should NEVER attend the audit or speak to the IRS without that tax professional right by their side. Jim missed an opportunity to clear up his tax case by not seeking professional help.

Despite the threatening letters, IRS audit agents are trained to be very friendly and concerned, making you feel comfortable and getting you talking about your life, family, and business. The point is, when people are "under audit," they often slip-up and reveal things that are not on the tax return. Jim was receiving cash for some construction work "under the table." With his money, he bought a $100,000 boat. Jim did not report the cash because he thought the cash was free money. The IRS disagreed.

The IRS wants to know how you can afford to live as you do, considering the income stated in your taxes. When the IRS finds a discrepancy, they will say that you committed fraud in either underreporting your income or overstating your expenses. Either or both of those may cause them to refer your case to an *IRS Criminal*

Special Agent. These are the people who are usually CPAs or equivalent, accountants, lawyers, and are highly trained for many years to look into businesses just like yours. Once again, Jim needed a tax professional representing him with the IRS.

Field Audits

Field audits are expensive for the IRS to conduct. They can take years and soak up large amounts of time and money. Previously, *Internal Revenue Agents* conducted these audits in your home and/or business. They sit at your dining room table or at a desk in your office. Due to Covid-19, they are not doing these in the field right now, but agents still will audit people on many complex issues by mail. An income tax audit by a *Revenue Agent* can yield on average $85,400. Lucky for you, the IRS only does about 250,000 of these audits a year. Clearly, it pays the IRS to do the complex audits, even if it's by mail. For example, if an IRS agent does ten audits a year at $85,000 return to the IRS, then they have made $850,000 for the US. The highest-level agents make around $150,000 in salary, pension, and benefits; thus, the net profit is $700,000.

When the IRS opens an audit on a Subchapter S corporation (real estate, restaurant, hair salon, etc.) or a "C" corporation (Amazon, Boeing, BP Oil, etc.), each member or shareholder may also be personally audited. The audit rate for these types of businesses is very low. It is only 0.22%, or one out of every 455 businesses. In 2018 there were only 10,670 audits out of 4.85 million corporations. But if you are selected for such an audit, you should hire a qualified tax professional immediately.

Lifestyle Audits

The IRS conducts audits to match your lifestyle/financial status with your living circumstances to what income you reported. For instance, if you have three houses and several cars along with a wealthy lifestyle and report an income of only $100,000 a year, it raises serious questions about how you can afford to do that. I worked on projects where we pulled information on high-dollar real estate transactions paid for in cash or with a large cash down payments; we also summoned car dealerships to get records on individuals who paid all cash for their cars. As a result of that investigation, we learned that the car dealerships were not reporting cash income, which led to charges against them. When people are living beyond their visible means, it can trigger an audit. This might be unbelievable, but Jim's brother-in-law reported Jim for his lavish lifestyle. Too bad Jim never made friends with his brother-in-law.

In Jim's case, he showed business losses of $80,000. Jim disclosed mortgage interest paid on a million-dollar house of $76,000; car payments on luxury cars of $35,000 while reporting a yearly income of only $40,000. The auditor asked Jim how he did that, and Jim became confused. Jim reported that they spent as much as he made and felt he should not even have to file income tax returns. (True story)

I always counsel anyone to report all of their income as required by law. Many tax benefits are available simply by filing tax returns. I have known some CPAs who advise their clients to at least report enough income to cover their known expenses. If the IRS can track you spending $15,300 a month, then you need to have an income of $15,300 a month. Be smart, not greedy.

The IRS looks at the numbers you reported on your return and looks at the credits, exemptions, and marital status. It judges whether they think that some information is inaccurate such as claiming a dependent that someone else has already claimed.

If you are claiming deductions for expenses, such as paying $100,000 a year in mortgage interest, but you report that you only earn $50,000, that is a problem. The IRS wants to know how you are paying bills and living a certain lifestyle when they cannot determine where the cash is coming from to make this happen. That can trigger an audit.

Alternatively, if you have a business and never make money or report expenses that are unusual compared to all the other businesses doing what you do, that can trigger an audit.

Audits always start with a letter in the mail, never by telephone. Audits conducted by mail are great because you never talk to the IRS.

The regular audits include *Earned Income Tax Credit* (EITC) audits. People who claimed the EITC have to present driver's licenses, marriage certificates, birth certificates, parenting agreements, divorce decrees, and school records that show they have the right to claim the dependents they're claiming. These audits hurt working people. Although there is fraud in every government program, EITC fraud is estimated to cost the US $18.4 billion a year, but that is minuscule compared to hundreds of billions that *Rich People, Big Businesses, and Corporations* cost the US utilizing tax loopholes to cheat the US of needed funds. Or as compared to the military budget.

The most audited tax returns are of the poor and working-class who receive the *Earned Income Tax Credit*. In 2019 39% of *Earned Income Tax Credit* recipients were poor or working poor. The five highest counties with the highest audit rates have a predominantly African-American population. These counties are located in the southern part of the United States.

The county with the highest audit rates is Humphreys County, Mississippi, where the median annual household income is $28,500. The IRS targets low-income families for auditing using the *Earned Income Tax Credit*, originally an antipoverty program, now used as a discriminatory program. I believe poorer Black and Brown skinned people are audited more than wealthy White people. This needs to stop now!

IRS Commissioner Charles Rettig said, "We are not biased on purpose when we audit 41% of EITC cases; it is just easier to do by mail." So, I say—why not just audit the *Rich People Big Businesses and Corporations* by mail also? Summons could be used to obtain what the IRS does not already know.

In 2021, in the midst of the Covid-19 pandemic, the working poor are audited at about the same rate as the wealthiest 1%. (Incomes over $538,926)

A critical question is for the lower-income workers—can they get their mail? Has Covid-19 cost them their lifestyle, house, and job?

Since 2011 audit rates for the wealthy have dropped more steeply than for the working poor. How is this fair? Paying taxes has become increasingly voluntary for those at the top and a desperate necessity for those at the bottom.

What Years Will My Audit Include?

As mentioned, audits are usually on tax returns two years back from the current year. For example, in 2022, they will be auditing 2019 and 2020 tax returns. It is not possible to make changes to your returns because they have already been filed. They cannot be amended during an audit. So, IRS is following up on whatever you reported. Again, I recommend you get a tax professional if you are audited. Do not represent yourself. If you made an error in one year, the IRS could expand your audit and can go one more year back and two more years forward. Jim is audited for 2019, and he made a mistake. The IRS can audit 2018 and 2020, and 2021. If IRS sends you a letter saying you owed $30,000 for one year, you will be audited for that same issue for additional tax years, i.e., lying about dependents. The additional taxes for those other years will be due, plus all sorts of penalties and interest. You will regret not just sending the check for the $30,000 because then the case would have been closed. You have no way to know about these things yourself; this is why you need to hire a tax professional.

Has an IRS Criminal Special Agent Contacted You?

IRS Criminal Special Agents work on cases of tax fraud, money laundering, and related criminal activities. They are able to review what you did two years ago or even twenty years ago. There is no statute of expirations on cases of fraud.

In 1995, the IRS Criminal Division employed 3,797 *Criminal Special Agents*. At the end of 2020, that number had plummeted by 47% to only 2,009 *Criminal Special Agents*. Presently my estimate is that there are 1,804 *Criminal Special Agents*. This is the lowest number of criminal investigators since 1971. Remember, the IRS is losing staff due to retirement and regular turnover every single day. 52,000 employees will retire or leave over the next six years. On July 6, 2021 the IRS announced that they would be hiring 500 new Criminal Special Agents in Fall, 2021. That is a start, at least.

IRS *Criminal Special Agents* do not maintain offices or have IRS agents in the States of Arkansas, Alabama, Connecticut, Iowa,

Idaho, Kansas, Kentucky, Louisiana, Maine, Minnesota, Mississippi, Montana, New Hampshire, New Mexico, Tennessee, Wisconsin, Wyoming, Utah, Vermont, Virginia, or West Virginia. Those states cases are worked by IRS *Criminal Special Agents* from surrounding states.

If you are being audited or owe the IRS, you may feel you are in a living hell for a while, but most likely, you will not do jail time. However, if you have income and do not file tax returns, then yes, you could be investigated by the *Criminal Investigation Special Agents*, and their goal is for you to be found guilty in court and go to jail. You do not want to commit fraud, bribery, or misrepresent your income; it is just not worth it.

Jim is one of 59 million gig workers. This means that he is an independent contractor, and he has agreements with "on-demand" companies. His kid brother, John, works for Uber, and Jim offers computer services. They both have the same problem. These men didn't pay their full share of taxes, and this has had two unfortunate results. First, Jim has compromised his Social Security pension by not filing and reporting his full income earned. John has also followed his brother's lead, so he too will have a smaller Social Security check when he needs the money the most. Secondly, Jim and John are now in trouble with the IRS; they have been contacted by a *Criminal Special Agent*. Anxiety laces their telephone calls between each other because there isn't enough money for a tax professional, and they don't want to go to jail. What can they do? To start, they need to read this book and carefully follow the steps to a successful encounter with an IRS agent.

The informal motto of IRS *Criminal Investigation* (CI) is "greed follows prosperity, and we follow greed." They will look for the most egregious cases of non-tax compliance and prosecute them. In 2013 they worked on 5,557 cases and referred 3,865 for prosecution. Of this, 3,311 were convicted of tax and financial crimes related to tax evasion, money laundering, and narcotics. IRS claims a 92% conviction rate. Yet, in 2019, CI only opened 2,797 criminal cases due to short staffing. In 2020 CI only opened 2,596 cases, and their conviction rate dropped to 79.8% due to short staffing.

A recent study showed that the 7% of income earners in the

bottom 50% of income earners had committed tax evasion. But the top 1% of income earners hide 21% through tax evasion. (NBER publication, John Guyton, Patrick Langetieg, Daniel Reck, Max Risch & Gabriel Zucman, Tax Evasion at the Top of the Income Distribution(NBER Working Paper Series No. 28542 March 2021), here.

Tax criminals usually receive 18 to 25-month sentences in federal prison. The chances of you getting caught are about the same as you winning the lottery. It is extremely rare, given that there were 253 million tax returns filed in 2019. If you are unlucky or extremely greedy and this happens to you, the mental, emotional, and health-related costs of a criminal investigation will depress, deplete, and could destroy you. Make good choices and pay your taxes.

You should hire a criminal tax attorney immediately if an *IRS Special Agent* contacts you. You will know who they are; they come in pairs and carry handcuffs and guns. They are very professional and friendly because they also want you to start talking and giving them additional information so they can send you to jail. Know that by the time they come out to interview you, they have already had your case for about a year and have all the proof they need. All they want to talk to you about is why it happened. They want to know what your "intent" was when you did what they are claiming that you did. Here is where you need professional advice.

Your criminal attorney will likely ask you for a $10-20,000 retainer to start the case because he already knows that you are in trouble if you are the subject of a federal case. Find the money and pay it! Please share this with people who need to hear it. It could save them some time in a six by eight-foot prison cell still owing the IRS money when they get out. Jim should have been honest!

CHAPTER 8
IRS SECRETS REVEALED

Information is liberating! The chapters in this book will tell you exactly how the IRS thinks and the agency's procedures. You will learn just enough information to protect your interests and get the best deal possible from the IRS.

The IRS treats its mission like a Janus coin—light on one side and dark on the other. On the light side, it wants to help taxpayers file and pay their taxes, but on the dark side, it assumes that most taxpayers are cheats and deserve to be exposed and punished. The IRS has secrets that could help people, but it is afraid to publish them for fear of making the taxpayers who do file and pay on time angry with the tax system that makes "deals." I can attest to this because I used to teach new IRS *Revenue Officers*.

Secret #1

You Do Not Need to File All Your Old Tax Returns

As of this publication date, the IRS will not usually ask for more than six years of tax returns from you. So, you only need to file tax years 2020, 2019, 2018, 2017, 2016, and 2015. That's it. Do not file 2014 or prior years because the IRS will not ask you for them. In 2022 you will not need to file your 2015 either. (Google—"IRS Policy Statement P-5-133") (I.R.M. 1.2.14.1.18)

Secret #2

You Can Reject IRS Prepared Tax Returns

Sometimes people are overwhelmed financially and in life. They stop filing taxes. If you stopped filing your taxes and the IRS has prepared a Form 1040 Income Tax Return for you under *Substitute for Return (SFR)* and *Automated Substitute for Return Process (ASFR)* under Internal Revenue Code §6020 (b) (see also IRM 4.12.1.25.3), You can go back and file your own version of Form 1040 and possibly get your tax, penalty, and interest greatly reduced. Let's break this down. Jim made $150,000 but didn't pay his taxes, and the IRS sent him a Form 1040 Income Tax Return stating he owed taxes on a gross income of $100,000. Jim has a choice. He can sign the form sent to him by the IRS, or he can file his own version of Form 1040. Then the trick is since Jim made $150,000 gross income and was only tagged for $100,000 gross income by IRS, he can sign the Form 1040 IRS sent him for $100,000, and this is now the new legal document. When he full pays that amount, then this IRS mistake yields him a huge bonus.

This also applies to businesses where the IRS has prepared their tax returns under the Internal Revenue Code 6020 (b) process. See also This is where the IRS estimates how much a business would owe for payroll taxes.

This is important to understand! Similarly, to Jim's situation, if the IRS shows a lower tax amount than what you would owe if you had filed a tax return, you can sign the consent form, which will become your legal tax. It's perfectly legal.

Secret # 3

The IRS wants to give you the best terms ever on your *Direct Deposit Installment Agreement (But is afraid to tell you about it!)*.

You can get an installment agreement for up to ten years if you owe $250,000 or less.

To apply for a *Direct Deposit Installment Agreement*, you

must request a *Form 433-D*. The IRS requires your bank name, routing number, and bank account number—all to be completed on *Form 433-D*. To make your own terms, just cross out the terms shown and write your own in. See Chapter 10 and Supplement G

Our man, Jim, has applied for a *Direct Deposit Installment Agreement* for his unpaid taxes. He completed Form 433-D. Jim set the length of the agreement he wanted (up to 10 years), he stated the amount he wants to pay and the date he wants to start making payments. Jim can do all of this without providing a financial statement to the IRS.

The suggested time limit to start paying is 60 to 90 days from application. Jim must assume that the IRS approves of his plan and start paying to avoid penalties. Jim must keep paying, or the IRS will file a *Notice of Federal Tax Lien* in his local county recorder's office, and this will affect his credit, but only if Jim owes more than $50,000.

Do you want to know what a Federal Tax Lien is? It is a lien everything you own now or acquire in the future; even a lottery ticket winning or an inheritance would be attached under this *Federal Tax Lien*.

Secret #4

Don't forget! You have the right to a reasonable installment agreement. Your agreement should be based on your current income and expenses. See Chapter 10.

Secret #5

You have the right not to pay your back taxes if doing so will cause you financial hardship. You must file and pay current taxes. You will have to prove why you have a hardship. See Chapter 11

You are allowed by law certain living expenses that the IRS cannot and will not question. You have the right not to pay your taxes if it will cause you financial hardship or deprive you of mental health or physical health care.

You have to prove your own hardship. You can use doctors' letters or medical records to support your how your mental or physical health problem(s)/treatment plan(s) prevent you from repaying your taxes.

Secret #6

You have the right to designate your voluntary payments to any tax module. The IRS always posts new payments to the oldest tax due period, which does not help you. You have the right to make additional payments outside your *installment agreement* at any time.

Sign up for the *Electronic Funds Tax Payment System* (EFTPS). This is important because using this system; you can designate exactly where the payments you make in the future will be applied.

Jim has an agreement with the IRS. Jim didn't designate the IRS to put his payments towards his current tax bill, and the IRS will put his payment on his oldest tax period. Now, poor Jim has penalties and interest on his current tax bill. He needs to take charge of his IRS commitments. If he doesn't understand this situation, he needs a tax professional.

Secret #7

Whatever agreement you make with the IRS, you must continue to be current in filing and paying your taxes.

Secret #8

Do not commit to an IRS-imposed installment agreement! Make your own.

You have no moral or legal obligation to repay your back taxes if it will cause you harm. IRS allowable expenses give you a set amount for your expenses, but many people do not understand them and strive to "do the right thing and pay their taxes or at least make payments on the old taxes." That is how they were raised. But if they have lost their income and cannot work for what they are worth, it is not their fault.

The IRS wants you to rejoin the taxpaying world and file and pay taxes now and into the future. Do the right thing for yourself so that you can do this. Once again, if you are confused, see a tax professional for your mental and physical health. Taxes never go away; they just accumulate.

Secret #9

After 10 Years, Your Tax Balance Will Disappear!

Any tax balance that you owe will expire ten years after the date of assessment. This is called the *Collection Statute of Expiration Date* (CSED), and it can be difficult to find, but here is how. Generally, you can estimate it. If you filed your 2010 taxes by their due date of 4/15/2011, then the assessment date was 4/15/2011, and the CSED date is 4/15/2021. On 4/15/2021, the tax balance from 2011 goes away forever.

The CSED date will give you hope and knowledge that you will no longer owe the unpaid taxes after that day. You can ask the IRS what that date is, or you can request a transcript. See IRS Get Transcript. You can also call me at 520-448-3531 or email me at richard@rmstaxconsulting.com. For a fee, I can help you.

Peace of mind comes from knowing that someday you will be free of the old tax debt forever.

Remember that if you file an appeal, bankruptcy, or an *Offer-in-Compromise*, these will all extend the *Collection Statute of Expiration Date* by six months plus the time that these functions are working your case. (See Chapter 10 for more details).

Let's return to Jim. Jim has filed an *Offer-in-Compromise* because he saw on TV that this was a neat way to help him with his tax problem. He now has 18 months before the IRS accepts or rejects his offer-in-compromise. So now Jim has ten years plus 18 months plus six months added to his CSED, so his tax problems will hang on for a much longer time. If Jim had seen a tax professional, he would have been advised against this approach.

Secret #10

Bankruptcy Gives You a Guaranteed Installment Agreement with No Penalties Interest, or it may Discharge all the Taxes.

If you owe income taxes and have not been able to pay them within three years of the date you received the first letter from the IRS (assessment date), you can file bankruptcy if you are insolvent, and then those taxes are erased. This does not apply to unpaid payroll taxes (*Trust Fund Recovery Penalty Taxes*—civil penalty).

Talk to a bankruptcy attorney for more information as the laws are complex.

Chapter 7 Bankruptcy is a liquidation bankruptcy. All of the debtor's non-exempt property is sold and distributed to creditors. This might be a good option for a person who has no assets, just debt and income under an amount that the courts find reasonable. Use Google or Bing to search Bankruptcy Chapter 7 Means Test. Then all debts are discharged (canceled) forever.

Chapter 11 Bankruptcy is a reorganization bankruptcy usually involving a business or an individual. This is where the debt is divided into different classes, and a payment plan begins to pay all creditors, at least in part. In this bankruptcy, some or all of the IRS penalties can be removed by the bankruptcy court.

Chapter 13 Bankruptcy allows an individual to consolidate their debt and make payments over a three-to-five-year period. Some of the debt is extinguished in the process, and the debtor can retain some or all of their property if they comply with the plan. Whether employed or self-employed, any individual may seek Chapter 13 protection so long as the individual's unsecured debts are less than $419,275 and secured debts are less than $1,184,200. Many people are unaware of this type of bankruptcy. If it is filed before an IRS lien in a bankruptcy situation, a taxpayer with higher income may benefit. A Bankruptcy Court Trustee will monitor their case.

In all three types of bankruptcies, the US Bankruptcy Court has acceptable monthly living standards and expenses, similar to the IRS National Allowable Monthly Expenses.

Income taxes but not unpaid payroll taxes (*Trust Fund Recovery Penalty* assessments) can be discharged in the following circumstances:

- If the tax debt is related to a tax return due at least three years before the taxpayer files for bankruptcy.

- The tax debt must be related to a tax return filed at least two years before the taxpayer files for bankruptcy.

- The tax assessment must be at least 240 days before the bankruptcy filing.

- The tax return was not frivolous or fraudulent.

- The taxpayer was not guilty of tax evasion.

Clearly, you will need to consult with a qualified bankruptcy attorney regarding your case.

Filing bankruptcy automatically stops any IRS collection actions. None of these three bankruptcies is an easy out. They will change people's lives and finances, sometimes painfully and in ways unwanted, but it can beat working with the IRS.

Secret #11

Show the IRS Why They Should Reduce or Remove Your Penalties

The IRS can be a big bully assessing poor people with huge penalties. But really, the IRS is just a paper tiger.

In 2019 the IRS assessed taxpayers with almost $40 billion in penalties. But they ended up taking away 5.4 million penalties amounting to $11,458,194. This is important! When the taxpayers challenged the penalties, the IRS backed down 13 to 30% of the time. This is another IRS secret. Never automatically accept and pay notices or adjustments from the IRS. Never! The IRS might be wrong or back down if you protest. The IRS admits to assessing penalties in error at least 20% of the time.

The IRS has the power to take away these penalties based on two circumstances:

(1) *First Time Delinquent Penalty Waiver,* where a taxpayer claims this was the first time, they had had this problem, and it was just one year. (See Internal Revenue Manual [IRM] 20.1.1.3.6.1 at *www.irs.gov*. Most penalties, but not interest, can be abated/removed).

(2) A second way is to claim *Reasonable Cause for Penalty Abatement.* This website explains how to establish that: www.irs.gov in IRM 20.1.1.3.2A. Then ask for the penalty to be abated/removed based on your reasons, such as:

- Your tax accountant told you bad information
- You suffered embezzlement from your bookkeeper
- You suffered from theft or loss due to a hurricane or another disaster such as death, illness, being out of the country or in jail, fires, casualty, civil disturbance, tornados, hurricanes, floods
- You suffered from an inability to get records needed to file returns

These are all causes for penalty abatement (removal). Many penalties can be abated when the IRS is in the mood to be reasonable. Jim had a plumbing business. He didn't pay his taxes because of lack of business during Covid-19, yet he kept his three workers on his payroll. He withheld taxes from his employees, but he never turned it over to the IRS. Now he is in big trouble with the IRS. The IRS sent him a letter. Jim went into a full depression episode and didn't reply to the IRS. He ignored the letters from the IRS. The letters explained his penalties and interest charges. As a result, the IRS put a lien on his property, and his wife's salary was garnished.

Although Jim was embarrassed, Jim needed to be frank with the IRS about his personal situation so that he could ask for the penalties to be removed. The IRS may be reasonable in Jim's situation. Covid-19 has created many "Jim's."

Here is another way to understand this. Many taxpayers are told by IRS employees that penalties cannot and are never removed or abated. Or taxpayers are told that they have to pay the penalty first and then file an *843 Claim Form*. But you have to ask for penalties to be removed. In the collection, they use a *Reasonable Cause Assistant (RCA) System*—this is supposed to take the subjectivity out of penalty abatement. In my experience, it is not accurate and is punitive with its determinations, and is wrong at least 70% of the time. No matter what the IRS employee tells you, the *Reasonable Cause Assistant* can be overruled. (IRM 20.1.1.3.6.10.1) at *www.irs.gov*. For instance, the IRS will abate penalties in cases of embezzlement, but the *Reasonable Cause Assistant* System states that embezzlements must have been discovered in six months for this to be allowed. What the IRS has in their tax programming is unfair, arbitrary, and capricious. This can still be appealed.

The bottom line is you have nothing to lose and the removal of the penalty amount to gain if you file an appeal asking for penalty abatement due to your circumstances. Anything that affected your life may be used to help get the penalties abated—your mental or physical health, your substance abuse—legal or illegal, etc.

The IRS has discussed Covid-19 penalty relief. If Jim had Covid-19, his job losses, reduced income, or hours would qualify Jim for the Covid-19 penalty relief. This also applies if other people in your house were sick or lost their jobs or income. **The key is to write Covid-19 on your 2020 tax return for tax relief consideration.**

The IRS is negligent in not promoting this. It does not advertise it anywhere on their computer system, www.irs.gov, or any information about "First Time Penalty Abatement" and "Reasonable Cause for Penalty Abatement." Knowing this secret can save you big money.

Secret #12

Just Because You Can Pay, Does Not Mean That You Should Pay

Just because you want to pay your back taxes doesn't mean that you should pay. That is why the IRS allows you a certain amount for your expenses whether you spend money on those expenses or not. Just because you have money today doesn't mean you will tomorrow. Don't over-commit. That is why the IRS has procedures for you to document your financial situation so that you can legally not pay your old taxes now or maybe even in the future based on your circumstances. See Chapter 11.

Jim is a realtor and has been successful in selling high-end properties. Joanie, his wife, had Covid-19 and died. Jim had to stay home and take care of their children; he suffered a nervous breakdown. Jim can no longer work. Jim can no longer pay the amount on his *installment agreement* with the IRS. The *Installment Agreement* will default, and a lien will be placed on his property. Jim needs to consult a professional who will help him start over with the IRS. If Jim had access to the IRS, he could have explained his situation and saved everyone time and money. See Chapter 11.

Secret #13

Secrets of the "Queue" and IRS Ranking

Currently, the IRS does not have enough employees or resources to work on all of their cases. So, if your case is not actively being worked and you do not have an installment agreement or a designation of *Currently Not Collectible Due to Financial Hardship*, then your case is:

- *In the Queue* (in the *Service Center Collection, Automated Collection System* [ACS] or the *Revenue Officer Queue*. This is a waiting place to see if an employee will become available to work the case. After 52 weeks, the case must leave the *Queue* and either go to another *Queue* or be *Shelved*.

- The case can be *Shelved*, which is exactly as it sounds; when they were paper, they used to be boxed up and sit on a shelf until they expired.

- The case can be *Surveyed by National Office*. This means bearing some unlikely event; the case never sees daylight again as long as you are filing and paying current taxes.

For most people, the more they owe the IRS, the less likely they are to be able to pay it. 66% of all collection cases are under $5,000. Most people owe under $50,000. This is the same amount you might spend on a nice car. If you paid it off over six years, you would have high payments, but you can pay the balance. Most of the individual balances due are for less than $50,000.

The Treasury Inspector General for Tax Administration reported that the IRS is very effective at collecting balances under $5,000 but not as effective collecting balances over $25,000.

These 13 secrets of the IRS are ones that should be discussed with a tax professional for your mental and physical health. You cannot buy health, but you can buy a professional to save your life.

Secret #14

Some individual taxpayers who haven't paid 2019 taxes and owe less than $250,000 may qualify to set up an installment agreement without having a *Notice of Federal Tax Lien* filed by the IRS. A *Notice of Federal Tax Lien* means the IRS will file a lien against any real and/or personal property in public records. Your credit is ruined. This is another major secret that the IRS does not share

Secret #15

The IRS sent out 40 million letters proposing penalties, but when taxpayers filed appeals, the IRS backed down and took away 11.4 million penalties. That is almost 30%; those taxpayers explained what happened, and the IRS backed down! This is another IRS secret. Never automatically accept and pay a notice or adjustment from the IRS. Never! The IRS might be wrong or back down if you protest. If you are uncertain, hire a tax professional with a solid reputation. IRM 20.1.1.3.2.1irs 20.1.5.1.6.1

For most people, the more they owe the IRS, the less likely they are to be able to pay it. 66% of all collection cases are under $5,000. Most people owe under $50,000. This is the same amount you might spend on a nice car. If you paid it off over six years, you would have high payments, but you can pay the balance. Most of the individual balances due are for less than $50,000.

The Treasury Inspector General for Tax Administration reported that the IRS is very effective at collecting balances under $5,000 but not as effective collecting balances over $25,000.

Secret #16—The Biggest Secret

The New Secret Installment Agreement

The IRS has issued a *Manual Deviation*—in English; this means that they are trying something new. They are giving away *Installment Agreements* with no financial statements or documentation. This has never happened before and is the whole reason that I wrote this book. This "New Deal" is explained below. It can be removed at any time, but it works as of the date of publication of this book. If this does not work then see Chapter 10 for more tradition installment agreement methods.

- To apply for this agreement, complete *Form 433-D Installment Agreement.* Pick any day of the month between the 1st and the 28th for your payment. Then make the first payment date 60 days into the future.

- You take the current balances from your IRS letters and divide them over up to 120 months. But practically speaking, the term ends when your ten-year expires. (CSED). This is always a hassle to find out what it is. In general, it will be on your oldest tax year due. Estimate that date. If you owe for 2015 Income taxes, the due date of that year's return was April 15, 2016. Add ten years to that, and that would be April 15, 2026. On January 25, 2021, that means that you have four years and four months left or 52 months. If you owed taxes for 2019, that return was due July 15, 2020; if you filed on time, then the expiration date would be July 15, 2030.

- You do not need to provide a financial statement: no *Form 433-A*, *Form 433-B*, or *Form 433-F*.

- The agreement must be a *Direct Debit Installment Agreement*. IRS needs your bank name, routing number, and account number

- On the form, you need to sign at the bottom and initial the box on the left side of the form halfway down.

- The IRS may file a *Notice of Federal Tax Lien* if you owe over $50,000.

- The IRS can withdraw its lien after you have made two months' worth of payments.

- That's it. See what is required of you before you qualify for the agreement and after you get the agreement.

- Just because there is the option to get this liberal agreement, you may not want to do this if you do not have adequate income to pay all your living expenses and have the standard of living that the IRS allows all taxpayers. See the *Currently Not Collectible* chapter for more details. (Chapter 11).

These 16 secrets of the IRS are ones that should be discussed with a tax professional for your mental and physical health. This book is intended to give you hope, knowledge, and just enough IRS procedural knowledge to get you good results in your tax case. If that fails, then you can always "rent" a tax professional to get you good results as well.

CHAPTER 9
HOW TO RESPOND TO THE IRS

> Never call the IRS (unless they have sent you a document that says they will levy/seize your wages or bank account).

First, you have to figure out if the letter you have in your hand is really from the IRS or if is a fraud. There are a lot of letters that appear to be from the IRS but are *actually fake*. Just read the letter. You might notice there are spelling errors, or it's not written in common English. For instance, the IRS refers to itself as the Department of the Treasury, not as the IRS that is a big clue. If you see incorrect terminology such as "Bureau of Internal Revenue" rather than IRS or the use of the words "Tax Warrant," then it is fake. Often this fraudulent letter tells you to call a phone number to talk to a person. You may hear a heavy accent telling you to pay your taxes by getting gift cards and sending the cards to them online. This is not how the IRS works.

Here is what a fraudulent letter looks like.

> **Distraint Warrant**
>
> This warrant has been issued against the above-named debtor (s) because of the tax debt that has not been paid in full. This isn't an arrest warrant. This warrant serves the same function as a court judgment. The Federal Tax Authorities uses the warrant in collection action, such as a garnishment of wages and bank accounts, property seizures, federal tax refund offset, and creation of a property lien.

> To avoid enforcement, call 1 (800) 719-1093. Levying procedures will being within 15 days of it's receipt. You must respond to the IRS, or we will send your local sheriff out there this afternoon to arrest you and take your children away from you.
>
> Copied from an actual letter—all English and Grammatical errors included.

How do you know you are speaking with the IRS?

If you suspect that the person calling you is not from the IRS or the letter you have received does not appear to be genuine, call the IRS directly at 1-800-829-1040 and report this fraudulent incident.

If you get a phone call and you think it may be an IRS agent, ask for the agent's employee identification number and then call the IRS at 1-800-829-1040 to verify the real agent contact. Trust your gut feeling!

You may have to wait on line, but at least you can verify that the IRS is trying to contact you. It can be frustrating because IRS does not pick up 75% of incoming calls. The important thing to know with the IRS letter or phone call is that the agency already knows most of your data. The IRS will try to confirm who you are by asking you pertinent questions. Unlike the fraudulent letters and phone calls, you will not be threatened that the sheriff is coming out to arrest you.

When you receive a **REAL** notice letter from the IRS, you have two options:

- Call the IRS using the phone number in the letter.
- Send a letter providing the IRS with additional request information.

My advice is don't ignore the letter and don't hope that the IRS will go away. The IRS may go quiet, but it never goes away.

Sadly, many people are afraid and don't respond to letters or follow-up phone calls from the IRS. They suffer from ensuing anxiety by not facing reality.

Before You Contact the IRS

You need to organize all your tax and financial income records and figure out the best way to present your case. You need to explain it to the IRS representative in a way that will cause the representative to understand your situation and, hopefully, help resolve it in your favor.

- You should gather the information they are requesting and photocopy it and then write a simple letter explaining your answer to the IRS letter and what proof you have of your position.

- Never send original documents, or the IRS will lose them.

- Your response to the IRS should be sent via certified mail. This does not get your case worked any faster, but it does prove that you mailed the requested information to the IRS address. If your letter is lost or destroyed by the IRS, this certification can make the difference between getting a seizure/levy on your wages or bank account lifted or not. Otherwise, the IRS will take the position that you did not respond at all. Hold onto your certified mail receipt!

With the IRS, you need to remember that their unofficial standard is, *"You are guilty until you prove yourself innocent of whatever the IRS is claiming you did wrong."*

You have to know what you want to achieve before you can figure out how to get it. For example, if the IRS is proposing to raise your taxes, you want to verify the taxes paid on your tax return, so the tax remains the same. This could be verifying that you are married or that your dependents are people you can legally claim on your tax return.

If you owe a tax balance, learn about your rights and/or contact a tax professional. To start, this may depend on how much you owe and for how many years you haven't paid taxes.

Is the IRS Always Right?

No. Just because you received a bill from the IRS does not mean that it is correct. First, check your records and see if you made an error on your tax return—see if the numbers were transposed or if you made a math error. However, these errors are increasingly rare because so many people use automated tax programs.

It may seem there is no rhyme or reason for how the IRS operates to you, a person outside of the IRS, but the IRS runs on procedures and manuals, so everything they do is part of an overall system. Everything eventually leads to your case being closed. Also, just because the computer sends you a letter does not mean that you owe the tax. Tax professionals suggest that the error rate is 5% to 20%!

IRS Letters

Although the IRS has tried to make some of its letters more understandable to its taxpayers, the letters are still confusing; they are six to ten pages long. For most people, it is hard to understand what the IRS wants or is instructing you to do. Before responding, review the letter several times to determine what it is asking for. A helpful hint is to Google: *Understanding My CP 2000, or CP504, or LT11*. Next, insert your letter number where indicated. This will take you to www.irs.gov and tell you everything that you need to know about why the letter was issued or what is required next.

All letters will address one of three areas:

- Directing you to do something—go to the office for an audit or to request receipts or other proof of what was on your return. Full pay your taxes.
- Asking you for more information.
- Requiring you to do something such as provide a financial statement or file a tax return by a certain deadline.

This can be confusing because the IRS often does not just specifically ask you about something that they are disputing in the letter.

The IRS letter will tell you that they have changed your return, and now you owe increased tax, penalties, and interest, all without waiting for you to respond. Many people do not even try to reply or fight what the IRS is presenting; they simply send a check thinking that this will stop further audits or collection actions.

Here is a case example: Jim got an IRS letter. The IRS letter requested more information on his tax return from two years ago and the receipts for his itemized deductions. Jim called and took down the agent's ID number. The agent asked specific questions before allowing Jim to present his case.

Jim is anxious because the letter has a deadline of 30 days, and he is supposed to go to Hawaii on vacation. The agent tells Jim that they have re-done his return, and he now owes penalties, interest, and tax for that year. Jim is horrified. He already paid for Hawaii, and without due consideration, Jim sends a check to the IRS, thinking this will prevent another audit.

Paying off an audit letter does not prevent future audits. Paying a collection amount for one year does not prevent future collection actions in other years.

The most important thing to remember is that you have the right to understand any changes that the IRS proposes making on your tax return.

It is imperative to respond to IRS letters and provide them with what they ask for. Keep things simple. Do not provide anything more than what they specifically request. Additional information might get the IRS employee interested in exploring your tax case more thoroughly, leading to a different outcome.

IRS Telephone Calls

Due to budget cuts by Congress, the IRS is seriously understaffed. Do not expect the IRS to make phone calls to taxpayers these days.

Here's How to Talk to the IRS:

Once you call the IRS, the IRS agent tells you their name and gives you their employee identification number. Write it down. Next in the structured interview, the agent will ask for your name, Social

Security number, date of birth, and adjusted gross income on your most recently filed Form 1040 Income Tax Return. Let the agent ask all the questions and respond only to the information requested. Be brief! Be clear and concise. Be courteous. Do not offer extraneous information. This conversation takes place all before you tell them why you are calling. This is an IRS process.

When the agent asks how they can help you, do not start the conversation by telling them how much you dislike the IRS or how many hours you were on hold before they answered your phone call. Additionally, don't complain about how many months/years you waited for someone to be assigned to work your case. This approach will start your experience with negativity.

The IRS employees are trained to do their jobs as best as they can. They want to resolve your case as quickly as possible. Collection work is frustrating for them too. They talk to taxpayers who are afraid to call the IRS, worried about what the IRS agent will tell them, and angry about the potential financial fallout from tax problems.

More advice, don't try to figure out where the IRS employee is coming from psychologically. Sometimes, your idle chatter upsets them. All you need to know is that they are under pressure to pick up the calls and close the cases. Some employees may sound almost robotic in their interviews with you. This is how they were taught to conduct the conversation. It is not a personal reflection of you.

On the other hand, instead of helping you, some IRS employees will judge you, blame you, and condemn you for your actions, inactions, or other choices. This is why you don't want to get into a power match with them. Stay relaxed, balanced, and professional. Focus on your case so that it is resolved in the best possible way for you. It might seem like they want to provoke you. Do not react. Remember, they have the power position over your financial future, mental and even physical health. Many IRS employees take a neutral, professional attitude as your tax issue is not their problem. It is your problem.

If you don't know the answer to a question that the IRS employee is asking, then don't make stuff up. **Never lie!** Tell them that you will have to find out the answer and get back to them in response to their question. It is better to give them actual, factual information, even if it means a second phone call. The IRS can give you a deal, but it may or may not be in your favor.

After you answer the initial round of questions asked of you, the IRS employee will automatically move on to additional questions, such as:

- Your home, cell, and work phone numbers.
- Name and address of the place where you work.
- Name of your bank and account number.

This can feel very intrusive, but in cases where the IRS claims you owe money, they have the right to ask this. Unfortunately, when you failed to pay your taxes, it is like inviting the IRS into your life for the next ten years. If your IRS conversation seems to be going in the wrong direction, hang up the phone! Regroup and write a letter instead. This may seem counter-intuitive, but it is important that you present your financial status accurately.

After discussing your case with the IRS, the IRS representative will decide how to resolve your case. It's as simple as that. You have one chance. Make *sure* that the agent understands your case, and you have revealed any special circumstances because that can help you. Petty excuses don't work. The way the IRS sees it, at some point, you had those tax dollars in your hand; it was your income, and you owed your taxes to the US The IRS believes you spent those dollars on something else instead of paying your taxes due as was your civic duty as a US citizen.

If the IRS doesn't offer you a reasonable solution, you have the right to speak to the representative's immediate manager. For audit cases, you have this right at any time. You can speak to the manager informally or file *Form 9423 Collection Appeal Request* for collection cases. The manager must call you within 24 hours to discuss your case. Should you choose this route, realize the 24-hour rule is stressful and could create a different scenario than you expected. This may or may not get you what you want. This means the manager understands the job better than you do. If you cannot find a solution you can live with, your case will be forwarded to an appeals officer.

Speaking to the IRS Person to Person

There are five ways that you may speak to an IRS agent person to person:

- Should you go to an IRS office for information or advice; you will meet employees who work in the *Taxpayer Assistance Center* (TAC) and are the first line of IRS customer/taxpayer service—Contact Your Local IRS Office, you should be able to find the nearest IRS office. Not all towns or even cities have a TAC. All TAC offices work on an appointment-only basis.

- The second is if you are told to appear at an IRS office for an office audit. You will speak to a *Tax Compliance Officer / Tax Auditor* (TCO), an employee who is required to have only limited accounting skills but is highly trained in IRS tax matters. They will audit some part of your Individual Income tax return/*Form 1040*. Some *Tax Compliance Officers* do have more experience or education than the job requires, so do not dismiss them or assume they don't know the law.

- The third type of contact will be a *Field Revenue Agent* (RA), who will come to your home or business and audit your personal or business returns. *Revenue Agents* have extensive accounting and tax law experience. Some also have master's degrees in Taxation or are Certified Public Accountants, or are lawyers.

- The fourth type will be a *Field Revenue Officer* (RO), who will come to your home or business to view and assess what you own and try to collect your tax balances from you based on the value of your assets.

- The fifth type is an IRS *Criminal Special Agent* (SA). The IRS always sends two agents for these cases. Dealing with a *Special Agent* can be the most dangerous contact you have. They have the power to arrest and jail you. Be polite, but ask to speak to your attorney first, and then stop talking! Anything you say can and will be used against you in a criminal case. The *Criminal Special Agent* refers their conclusions for the prosecution to the US Attorney, which is part of the Department of Justice (DOJ).

Final Thoughts

Be patient. Organize your records. Understand the process and see a tax professional if you are confused, in doubt, or need another set of ears.

CHAPTER 10

HOW TO GET THE BEST INSTALLMENT AGREEMENT FROM THE IRS

The IRS is offering the best *installment agreement* terms it ever has, but the IRS likes to keep its secrets as usual. This information is not published anywhere on the IRS website and is not in the IRS laws! It's a secret that only tax professionals know about it.

This is where the book gets complicated because the IRS makes things complicated. The IRS is the bully on the playground; it will show everyone how tough it can be. Of course, that makes it hard for you to resolve your case with them. And because of Covid-19 and the fact that the government spends more than it takes in and owes $30 trillion in national debt, the IRS needs to collect a lot more money for the government to spend.

Due to the letter sent to you from the IRS, you already know what the IRS thinks that you owe. There are also added penalties, and interest tacked onto that amount. This is what you need to question. Maybe the penalties are valid, and maybe not. What do you think? Do you understand and agree with the tax, penalties, and interest?

The Tax Amount

What you owe came from either your original tax return, your amended tax return, from an IRS-created tax return, or an IRS adjustment that adds taxes to your account.

Penalties and Interest

Some penalties can be removed for two reasons. (1) *First Time Penalty Abatement Waiver*, you have not owed taxes in the last three years. (2) Things were happening beyond your control in your life, and that caused you not to file or pay your taxes. *(Reasonable Cause for Penalty Abatement)* However, if you are not ever going to pay your taxes fully, don't even bother trying to get penalties removed; it won't make any difference in the end. Additionally, although interest is rarely removed, it is possible to get it reduced when your overall balance goes down.

If you disagree with some of the penalties or interest, the next chapter will go into more detail.

Do You Understand What You Owe and Why?

You have to figure out where you fit in the IRS system. If you understand and agree with paying the tax balance, interest, and penalties, we move to the next level.

To get the best deal from the IRS, you need to figure out where your case is in the IRS system. All cases start in an *IRS Service Center Collection (The Pipeline)*. You know this because this is the place that is sending you all those letters. Your tax return is received, and date stamped and assessed. The assessment date starts the ten-year period where you will legally owe the tax. That date can be extended by bankruptcy or filing an *Offer-in-Compromise*, but for most people, the remainder of owed taxes goes away after ten years. The Service Center generates a letter to you, starting your case through the *IRS Pipeline System*. If your case is not resolved at the Service Center after 52 weeks, it is transferred to the *Automated Collection System (ACS) Queue* or *Shelved,* where the case waits to be assigned into active ACS inventory. Or it can go to the *Revenue Officer Queue.*

Chapter 10: How to Get the Best Installment Agreement from the IRS

Can You Pay or Not Pay?

Those who cannot pay are the unemployed, underemployed elderly, unemployable, sick, or unable to earn what they once did or if they have lost their business. If you can pay, the IRS has many different *installment agreement* payment options depending on:

- Where your case is assigned in IRS.
- The amount of the balance you owe.
- The type of taxes that you owe—income or business or both.
- If you can pay in the short term or long term.

What Can Happen Without an Installment Agreement?

The IRS will send collection letters that grow increasingly threatening. These letters inform a taxpayer that the IRS may levy (seize) bank accounts, brokerage accounts, wages, salary, and other income. This can include payments from the federal government for Social Security and federal pensions, subject to an automatic 15% deduction through the *Federal Payments Levy Program* (FPLP). As you are learning, IRS uses fear and threats that they are going to take all of your stuff to force "voluntary" compliance.

If you do not pay, you can expect the IRS to levy/seize your:

- Bank accounts
- Wages, salary, and any other income
- Your house, vacation house, rental house
- Cars, trucks, boats, RV's, campers
- Stocks, bonds, dividends
- Business income
- Current and future tax refunds
- Social Security or disability check or annuities
- Inheritances

- Interests in corporations, partnerships, trusts, or estates
- Lawsuit proceeds
- Business equipment not otherwise exempt
- Retirement accounts which include 401(k), IRA, Keogh, SEP
- Pensions and profit-sharing plans. The IRS cannot force you to withdraw money from your pension plan. It cannot assign a value to something that you cannot withdraw or are not old enough to qualify for a benefit from.
- If you close an IRA to pay your taxes, you pay tax on that and a 10% penalty. If the IRS seizes the IRA, there is no penalty. You can encourage the IRS to issue a levy to seize your IRA and save you the 10% penalty
- Anything else you own
- You can also lose your passport if you owe tax, penalties, and interest of more than $50,000.
- A Federal Tax Lien may be filed for balance due amounts.
- If the delinquent tax balance due is over $51,000, a new IRS program threatens to suspend or revoke a taxpayer's US passport. Taxpayers have received CP 508-C letters from the IRS showing that they owed the US State Department.

This can be reversed when a taxpayer has an approved Installment Agreement, or their case is found to be Currently Not Collectible.

Other Options to Resolve Your Case

A small percentage of cases are resolved through the IRS *Offer in Compromise* Program, bankruptcy, or *IRS Appeals*.

Cases Assigned to a Field Revenue Officer

If your case has been assigned to a *Field Revenue Officer* (tax collector) or is in the "Queue" for a *Revenue Officer,* the options discussed above do not apply.

Make Payments Without an Agreement

You can always make voluntary payments to the tax years and periods you chose using the *Electronic Funds Transfer Payment System* (EFTPS).

The Easy Way to Pay IRS Without Talking to the IRS

IRS Collection is now offering more liberal installment agreement options to taxpayers who know how to find them.

The New Secret Installment Agreement

The IRS has issued a *Manual Deviation*—in English; this means that they are trying something new. They are giving away *Installment Agreements* with no financial statements or documentation. This has never happened before and is the whole reason that I wrote this book. This "New Deal" is explained below.

- To apply for this agreement, complete *Form 433-D Installment Agreement.* Pick any day of the month between the 1st and the 28th for your payment. Then make the first payment date 60 days into the future.

- You take the current balances from your IRS letters and divide them over up to 120 months. But practically speaking, the term ends when your ten-year expires. (CSED). This is always a hassle to find out what it is. In general, it will be on your oldest tax year due. Estimate that date. If you owe for 2015 Income taxes, the due date of that year's return was April 15, 2016. Add ten years to that, and that would be April 15, 2026. On January 25, 2021, that means that you have four years and four months left or 52 months. If you owed taxes for 2019, that return was due July 15, 2020; if you filed on time, then the expiration date would be July 15, 2030.

- You do not need to provide a financial statement: no *Form 433-A*, *Form 433-B*, or *Form 433-F*.
- The agreement must be a *Direct Debit Installment Agreement*. IRS needs your bank name, routing number, and account number
- On the form, you need to sign at the bottom and initial the box on the left side of the form halfway down.
- The IRS may file a *Notice of Federal Tax Lien* if you owe over $50,000.
- The IRS can withdraw its lien after you have made two months' worth of payments.
- That's it. See what is required of you before you qualify for the agreement and after you get the agreement.
- Just because there is the option to get this liberal agreement, you may not want to do this if you do not have adequate income to pay all your living expenses and have the standard of living that the IRS allows all taxpayers. See the *Currently Not Collectible* chapter for more details. See Chapter 11.
- You can only get this agreement on cases in the *Service Center Collection Pipeline* and in the *Automated Collection System*.
- *If you owe $250,000 or less for Individual Income Taxes, Trust Fund Recovery balances, and out-of-business sole proprietors tax balances:*
- You can get up to 120 months (up to the *Collection Statute of Expirations*) (CSED)
- You can make an *Installment Agreement* with no financial statement.
- *Notice of Federal Tax Lien* on balances over $50,000, but this can be removed during the term of the agreement if it is direct debit.

Chapter 10: How to Get the Best Installment Agreement from the IRS

- It must be a direct debit agreement from your bank account.
- Apply on Form 433-D Installment Agreement.

What is the Automated Collection System (ACS)?

Cases worked by *Automated Collection System* employees range from $50,000 to $250,000. ACS employees cannot work cases over $250,000.

Some ACS employees are not aware of the above "special deal" from the IRS. Their job is to make you have an installment agreement that fits the Governments' terms, not your budget. At this point, you may need to remind the employee of the "special deals" available.

Many people cannot even pay at all but are intimidated into an agreement.

Automated Collection System employees answer incoming calls from taxpayers and discuss the taxpayer's debt to prompt payment or set up a payment plan that the IRS calls an *Installment Agreement* (IA). ACS staff may also take enforcement actions, such as seizing (levying) bank accounts, wages, and other income. Alternatively, they may file a lien against the taxpayer's property. In 2018, ACS resolved 5,000,000 cases (23% of total collection inventory).

Automated Collection Systems employees are on a lower pay scale and have less specialized knowledge about tax procedures and tax laws. Callers will never speak to the same ACS employee twice; the system is not designed that way. ACS employees work correspondence from taxpayers and only answer the calls of taxpayers responding to IRS collection letters. Currently, they no longer make outgoing collection calls. If ACS cannot resolve the case within 52 weeks, it will either be Shelved or sent to the *Field Collection Queue* (Field) for assignment to a *Revenue Officer*.

What are *Surveyed,* *Queued,* or *Shelved* Cases?

A *Surveyed* case is one where the IRS computer reviews all cases using a "secret case selection criteria." Then it decides that it cannot afford to spend any time working on that case at all. These are cases that the IRS has decided that it will not work for two reasons: (1)

They will yield "little or no tax." (2) IRS does not have the budget or employees to work these cases. There are millions of cases that the IRS will never work even though the taxpayers owe them money. Generally, this is for amounts under $10,000 or for unfiled returns that will yield little in taxes. These cases that the IRS end up in being *Shelved* or *Queued*.

One clue in the Internal Revenue Manual listed under Transfer Service Center to *Automated Collection System* or *Shelved* does list that "low dollar" balances due (under $10,000) will not be transferred to ACS or the Field. That is because recent laws and procedures by Congress require the I.R.S to transfer these cases to a "private collection agency for collection." Yes, that is right, read it again. The Congress is contracting out one of the most basic functions of government—tax collection. Is this right? Is it political? Tests show that private tax collection agencies have a history of taxpayer abuse, violating their rights, and result in higher costs and less taxes collected than if the IRS had done the job.

It is helpful to understand more about the number of cases that are in the various *Queue* files. Cases stay in each *Queue* for only 52 weeks before being assigned to a different *Queue*—such as the *Service Center Queue*, the *Automated Collection System Queue*, or the *Collection Field Group Queue*. All cases worked by the Field are assigned based on the taxpayer's legal address (as reported to IRS) and zip code. If a case has not been assigned or worked after 52 weeks, it is *Shelved*. As it sounds, boxes of these cases used to just sit on shelves, never to be touched again.

You cannot request that your case be put into the *Queue, Surveyed,* or *Shelved*.

If a case is not resolved at the Service Center after 52 weeks, it is either *Surveyed, Shelved*, or is transferred to the *Queue*, where the case waits to be assigned into active *Automated Collection System* inventory. When cases are *Shelved*, it is under orders from the IRS National Office. In Fiscal Year (FY) 2015, there were 7.6 million cases *Shelved*.

IRS did not respond to my inquiry to tell me how many cases are in the various *Queue Files* or have been *Shelved*. I was told that it is

Classified Data. I am filing a *Freedom of Information Act Request* (FOIA) for this data and will publish it when it is released to me.

During the Time a Case is in the "Queue"

- Taxpayers will continue to receive the *CP71 letter (Annual Balance Due Reminder Notice)* reminding them of their balance, and

- Future tax refunds will be seized and applied to the oldest existing tax debt, and

- The *Collection Statute of Expiration* (CSED) does not toll, and it continues to run, and the tax balance will still expire after ten years.

- The case can be reissued at any time if future income tax returns indicate that income has risen.

Stop Worrying About Your Very Old Case

The Internal Revenue Manual also points out that cases will not be worked when the *Collection Statute of Expiration Date* (CSED) expires within two years and will not be issued to the *Automated Collection System* or *Field Revenue Officers*. Eventually, all cases that are not otherwise resolved within ten years will be *Shelved* permanently.

Service Center Collection-The Pipeline-Installment Agreements (IA) Under $50,000

The IRS offers *Streamlined IA's*. These Direct Debit agreements are for balance due cases of $100 to $50,000. These cases are assigned to Service Center Collection Pipeline.

Virtually every taxpayer who owes less than $50,000 qualifies for a *Streamlined Agreement*. These involve no IRS financial review or interaction with an IRS employee. You can apply online at https://www.irs.gov/payments/online-payment-agreement-application. Or using pen and ink, apply on Form 9465 *Installment Agreement Request* and mail it in.

Installment Agreement (IA) Pre-Qualifications Apply to All Cases

Before any taxpayer can request an *installment agreement*, they must:

- File all delinquent tax returns for the last six years.
- Have sufficient tax withheld or be current with estimated tax deposits in the current year.
- Be aware that any future tax refunds will be applied to the outstanding balance due.
- Not be in Bankruptcy.
- Not have filed an *Offer in Compromise*.
- Know that a one-payment automatic skip-payment is built into the installment agreement. (No notice is required to the IRS)
- Know that if they fail to file or pay their taxes in the future, it will cause the IA to default and lead to levies (seizure) of bank accounts and levies on their wages, salary, or other income.

All IA's come with *Installment Agreement User Fees* (IAUF) ranging from $31 to $225. Lower-income taxpayers can apply for a reduced user fee.

Form 9465 Online Installment Agreement

Form 9465 is an online interactive form. *Direct Debit Online Installment Agreement* requests under $50,000 and only providing limited financial data, with no *Collection Information Statement* (CIS). This form will give you an automatic 72-month installment agreement unless you request a shorter IA.

- No *Collection Information Statement* (CIS) is required if the taxpayer agrees to make payment by direct debit or payroll deduction.
- No *Notice of Federal Tax Lien* (NFTL) is required, but IRS may determine that filing a notice of federal tax lien would be in the Government's best interests.

Chapter 10: How to Get the Best Installment Agreement from the IRS

However, if the case is not a *Direct Debit Installment Agreement (DDIA)*, then an NFTL is required.

- **These terms do not apply to cases being worked by *Field Revenue Officers*.**

Automated Collection System Installment Agreements | Installment Agreements (IA) for $50,000 to $250,000

Officially, the way to get an *installment agreement* for balances due in this amount requires you to complete a *Form 433-A Individual Financial Statement* and *Form 433-B Business Financial Statement*. Your expenses will be reviewed and judged by the IRS. This is what IRS shows on its website. To negotiate an agreement like this is like shooting yourself in the foot.

See Chapter 10 for how the existing system works. Then do it the way I suggest instead.

The New Secret Installment Agreement

The IRS has issued a ***Manual Deviation***—in English; this means that they are trying something new. They are giving away *Installment Agreements* with no financial statements or documentation. This has never happened before and is the whole reason that I wrote this book. This "New Deal" is explained below.

- To apply for this agreement, complete *Form 433-D Installment Agreement*. Pick any day of the month between the 1st and the 28th for your payment. Then make the first payment date 60 days into the future.

- You take the current balances from your IRS letters and divide them over up to 120 months. But practically speaking, the term ends when your ten-year expires. (CSED). This is always a hassle to find out what it is. In general, it will be on your oldest tax year due. Estimate that date. If you owe for 2015 Income taxes, the due date of that year's return was April 15, 2016. Add ten years to that, and that would be April 15, 2026. On January 25, 2021, that means that you

113

have four years and four months left or 52 months. If you owed taxes for 2019, that return was due July 15, 2020; if you filed on time, then the expiration date would be July 15, 2030.

- You do not need to provide a financial statement: no *Form 433-A*, *Form 433-B*, or *Form 433-F*.

- The agreement must be a *Direct Debit Installment Agreement*. IRS needs your bank name, routing number, and account number

- On the form, you need to sign at the bottom and initial the box on the left side of the form halfway down.

- The IRS may file a *Notice of Federal Tax Lien* if you owe over $50,000.

- The IRS can withdraw its lien after you have made two months' worth of payments.

- That's it. See what is required of you before you qualify for the agreement and after you get the agreement.

- Just because there is the option to get this liberal agreement, you may not want to do this if you do not have adequate income to pay all your living expenses and have the standard of living that the IRS allows all taxpayers. See the *Currently Not Collectible* chapter for more details. (Chapter 11).

Collection Field Function—Revenue Officers

The *Revenue Officer* can work any case for any dollar amount. If taxpayers owe over $250,000 and do not respond to IRS letters, then their cases are forwarded to the *Field Collection Queue*, where they await transfer to *Field Revenue Officers* (R/O's).

All cases over $250,000 must be assigned to the *Field Collection Queue*. The good news for you is that there are only 1,776 *Revenue Officers* left in the IRS. So, it is very unlikely that you will ever hear from a *Revenue Officer*. Negotiating with the *Revenue Officer* is not to be taken lightly. It all comes down to the financial numbers being presented to the IRS and the proposal's reasonableness. *Revenue Officers* can negotiate *installment agreement* terms, but all results must be based on each taxpayer's financial situation.

The cases that are reissued with the highest priority in collection are those where the IRS has made an IA and the taxpayer has defaulted. Egregious cases, cases with a broad public impact, or have criminal aspects will still be issued quickly to a *Revenue Officer*.

You Have Successfully Negotiated an Installment Agreement—What Could Go Wrong?

OK, you have negotiated a reasonable IA for yourself; you are making current tax payments and filing their tax returns. What could go wrong? Anything anytime would be a safe answer. For instance, the IRS can:

- Send a letter proposing to terminate a taxpayer's *installment agreement Notice of Intent to Terminate Your Installment Agreement* (CP523) if the taxpayer does not submit new financial information within ten days.

- The IRS to review IA's every two years if the taxpayer's payment will never fully pay their IRS debt in the ten years before the *CSED* expires.

- See if the taxpayer's income has substantially increased. Suppose you get this letter to respond with a new *Collection Information Statement (Form 433-A)*. If you cannot do that within ten days, immediately write them a letter requesting an additional 30-45 days to compile new financial information. This will buy you some time. When you send that letter, it will trigger an IRS response that will tell you that you should hear back from the IRS in 30-60 days; this is an automatic process. The case review can result in the IA payment staying the same, being reduced, or the case may become *Currently Not Collectible* (CNC).

For instance, a taxpayer knows that he will not be able to file and pay his current year's tax return by April 15. So, he has the legal right to file for a six-month legal extension. He does file the return by the new October 15 deadline and pays all the money he owes. So, the taxpayer thinks that he complies.

The fact that the tax was not fully paid by April 15 places the account in default. But no IRS employee is looking at the account. When the *failure to file penalty* (TC 166-Delinquency Penalty) is assessed, and the failure to pay tax penalty is assessed on the late balance, it automatically triggers the *Intent to Default Your Installment Agreement Letter. (CP 523)* The taxpayer can offer to pay the penalty and contact the IRS to reinstate the agreement. Or it can default the agreement if their financial circumstances have changed.

Taxpayers also receive an annual *Reminder of Tax, Penalty and Interest Due Letter (CP 71A)* letter from the IRS, required by law to remind taxpayers that they still owe a balance due. That is independent of everything else we are talking about. Taxpayers can always ignore this letter; it is just information, not asking that the taxpayer take any actions. This letter is ill-conceived because it generates tens of thousands of calls every year and produces nothing but trouble for the IRS.

Changing or modifying an Existing Installment Agreement

Taxpayers are still in *Installment Agreement* (IA) status until the time that the IRS cancels it. The IRS may propose to terminate, but then a taxpayer can file an appeal, and *Appeals* will hear the case. Even when the IA is terminated, the taxpayer has sixty days to file an appeal that disputes the termination and requesting that their case is assigned to an IRS.

Appeals Officer. The IRS cannot levy a taxpayer if their case is in the *Appeals Division*. It may be in *appeals* one to three years. The *Appeals Officer* will usually be more reasonable than the *collection employee* because they have much higher levels of training, education and are well paid for their work. They dislike collection casework anyway because it is not glamorous. Taxpayers can speak directly to their *Appeals Officer*, and their case is permanently assigned to that person.

It is not normally possible for a taxpayer to terminate a direct debit IA. The IRS claims all taxpayers have to do is write or call the IRS and modify the agreement's terms. The only way to do this is by closing the bank account tied to the direct debit agreement. That is why it is always better to open a brand-new bank account just to be used for the *Direct Debit Agreement*.

It is very difficult to call or contact the IRS and include new tax balances on an existing agreement. Most taxpayers end up going through the default process and then have to resubmit financial information and renegotiate the agreement from scratch.

IRS IA's have a default rate that ranges from 28% for individuals to 70% for *In-Business Installment Agreements*. This is because their financial circumstances have changed, and they can no longer afford to pay. Sometimes the default is the taxpayer's fault, and sometimes it is due to the IRS being unclear about what the taxpayer will be required to do in the future.

Never Call the IRS Unless They Have Seized Your Bank Account or Wages

When you contact the IRS, you might just be asking what your options are. You might barely be paying your expenses, and you cannot pay anything more. However, during your conversation with the IRS employee, you may say the wrong things and get trapped into an *Installment Agreement* that you cannot afford. I have seen it hundreds of times. If the phone call is not going your way, hang up!

Your Tax Balance and the Notice of Federal Tax Lien (NFTL)

If you agree with the balance due, it is always better to pay it or borrow the money instead of installing an IRS *Installment Agreement*. That is because in cases where over $50,000 is owed, the IRS will file a *Notice of Federal Tax Lien*, which is a lien against you, your name, your real estate, your automobile, and any other assets or income that you have or come into in the future.

In cases where *Notices of Federal Tax Liens* are filed, 21% of taxpayers have never talked to the IRS, and there has been no review of their finances or circumstances. The NFTL is a public notice that you owe money, and that is scary. Friends, relatives, neighbors, creditors, co-workers, and anyone else will be able to look into your financial affairs and talk about you and your taxes. Worse yet, right after the lien is filed, you will receive dozens of letters and phone calls from predatory tax firms who will claim they want to represent you and will charge you a lot of money to do that.

If a *Notice of Federal Tax Lien Form (668Y)* is filed by *ACS or Field Collection*, you will receive a copy of it and a copy of Letter *3172—Notice of Federal Lien and Right to Collection Due Process Hearing*.

If you miss the 30-day deadline, you can still file a *Collection Due Process (CDP)* for an *Equivalent Hearing*. However, this does not freeze any pending collection actions.

In both cases, you also have the right to file a *Collection Appeals Request* (CAP), which is the right to talk to the employee's manager taking action against you. If you cannot reach an agreement with their manager, then your case will be forwarded to *Appeals* for their review. Use Google to search for *Form 1660—Hearing Available Under Collection Appeals Program*. Personally, I have never found those to be very productive because the manager is just another employee who used to do collection work, so he is likely to share the same attitudes. You have the right to file a CAP before or after a lien or levy is filed or after a seizure has taken place when your *Installment Agreement* has been denied or terminated. This temporarily stops Collection. Use *Form 9423 Collection Appeal Request* to start this process.

CHAPTER 11

CURRENTLY NOT COLLECTIBLE— WHEN YOU CANNOT PAY YOUR BACK TAXES NOW OR EVER

The IRS needs to do more to identify which cases are not going to be collectible now or in the future. Inside the Internal Revenue Service we used to be told by management that "service" is in our name. Year after year the IRS talks about "service" but what they do is not "service". It can be defined as more and more enforced collection activity. Actually, the IRS is very aggressive in its actions against people who owe under $100,000. The continuing stream for the delinquent taxpayer of IRS collection letters never ask why you owe the back taxes and if you can pay them. They never ask you what circumstances contributed in your life that prevent you from repaying your old taxes. They only demand and harass you with increasingly threatening letters. This is not fair to those taxpayers who have hit a rough patch in their lives. This chapter offers some suggestions for those taxpayers.

If you cannot pay, you have to provide a financial statement (*Collection Information Statement—Form 433-A* and *Form 433-B*) but there is no place on this six-page form that asks "how you got to this place." It doesn't ask where you are in your life now. The IRS needs a new form that can be attached to the financial statements where you tell your financial, emotional, mental or health or physical circumstances that are causing your hardship. If you clearly cannot pay, then the IRS needs to close your case and move on to other cases according to IRS *Policy Statement P-5-2* that states, "Case resolution, including actions such as lien, levy seizure of assets, installment agreements, offer in compromise, substitute for return, summons, and IRS 6020 (b) are important elements of an effective compliance program. When it is appropriate to take such actions, it should be done promptly, yet judiciously, and based on the facts of each case."

This also applies to determining when a hardship situation exists. When a taxpayer is not able to make monthly payments and maintain a reasonable standard of living then the IRS needs to judiciously step away from collections. It may seem great that the IRS is opening up and willing to grant installment agreements to taxpayers without contracting the IRS or requiring a financial statement. This is not good for most people! It does not take into account the guarantee that Congress intended for each taxpayer to have a minimal and reasonable standard of living. For this guarantee to apply, you have to complete financial statements. You have to make a written statement of the facts in your life, and be completely open in doing so. It will benefit you. The *Currently Not Collectible Due to Financial Hardship* status is determined based on the taxpayer's inability to pay the tax liabilities while paying necessary living expenses.

The IRS must stop collection action if it results in economic hardship. You must mention that and then be able to prove it.

In 2018, the IRS reported that there were 2.9 million *installment agreements*. 72% of them were *streamlined* which means that taxpayers never spoke to an IRS employee. These agreements did not require financial analysis and the taxpayers were never offered their right to the *Allowable Living Expense* (ALE) standards. This effectively denied taxpayers their rights to a basic standard of living. In fact, 40% of the taxpayers who made such agreements had no ability to pay the *installment agreement* because it caused them financial hardship. According to Nina Olson, the Taxpayer Advocate, she said, "This is criminal"!

The IRS instructions to its employees provide little direction to prevent undue economic hardship on affected taxpayers. There is

Chapter 11: Currently Not Collectible—When You Cannot Pay Your Back Taxes...

no attempt to prevent economic harm when the mindless IRS computer issues the bank and wage levy notices. *Economic hardship comes from the Internal Revenue Code §6343 and Internal Revenue Manual* (IRM) procedures are found in *IRM 5.19.4.4.10 (j)*. These adequately explain economic hardship. The major problem this wisdom is applied only after a levy is issued. The IRS does not ask or care about your economic hardship until and unless you bring it up. Again, this is wrong!

The *Internal Revenue Manual* (IRM) states that each case should be evaluated on three criteria: cooperation, current compliance, and good faith efforts. The more willing the taxpayer is to cooperate with the IRS and their desire to resolve their tax debts, even if they cannot pay them is crucial. The IRS is often the problem as well. The IRS has been forced to allow the tax problems to fester—sometimes for many years due to budget cuts and a shortage of employees.

I understand the need for the IRS to use its powerful collection tools to help administer the national tax laws. However, the IRS should reserve the use of these intrusive tools for uncooperative taxpayers who refuse to voluntarily file and pay their taxes when they have the ability to do so.

There is nothing new about this idea. Congress has directed the IRS to be fair and equitable and the IRS *Policy Statements* have incorporated this into IRS goals. The IRS employee training in the procedures and directions is where the failure occurs

By personally interacting with a taxpayer, even if it is done through correspondence, the taxpayer can share their facts and circumstances so that the IRS can decide what is available for collection options prior to issuing levies and liens. This will reduce the taxpayer burden and the economic hardships that would result if the taxpayer gets into an *installment agreement* that they can ill afford.

The IRS needs a new form where taxpayers can write about their finances and personal circumstances, mental and physical health and state why they are unable to full pay, borrow or make any payments currently without creating a financial hardship on them. They should attach this to their *Collection Information Statements*. A fair appraisal by the IRS would identify many taxpayers who cannot pay right now; or are also unlikely to be able to pay in the future. This should uncover a large number who also would instantly qualify for an *Offer in Compromise*.

What You Need to Know If Your Case is Uncollectible

- A *Collection Information Statement* (CIS) (IRS *Form 433-A* and *433-B*) are required by the IRS before *Currently Not Collectible* (CNC) is granted. The CIS requires the taxpayer to disclose income, assets and expenses. Some of the information may be verified by the IRS. Initially this includes bank statements for the last year.

- The Internal Revenue Manual states, "Generally, these cases involve no income or assets, no equity in assets or insufficient income to make any payment without causing hardship". Due to age and infirmity of the taxpayers, the IRS does not require the equity to be paid over to the government. Grounds for the IRS not requiring the taxpayer to get a loan against their equity in an asset is found in *IRM 5.16.1.2.9(6)*: "If the taxpayer has equity in assets, the reason collection is not being pursued must be documented in the history."

- A *Notice of Federal Tax Lien* will be filed when the unpaid tax balance exceeds $10,000.

- In proving that you can't pay, the IRS has to immediately release any wage or bank levies.

- The IRS requires that you file and pay any current taxes and taxes that arise in the future. However, in certain cases the IRS has the discretion to not require this if the *Currently Not Collectible* (CNC) is *Unable to Locate* or *Unable to Contact*. This is where the IRS cannot find you or has found you but you do not respond at all. They cannot attach liens/levies to any of your income sources perhaps because you are self-employed and have no bank account.

Chapter 11: Currently Not Collectible—When You Cannot Pay Your Back Taxes...

- The tax remains and continues to accrue penalties and interest for the full ten years that you owe the taxes.
- Interest and penalties continue to accrue while an account is in CNC.
- You will lose any future refunds during the time that you owe the taxes up the ten-year *Collection Statute of Expirations Date* (CSED).
- Hardship cases can be reactivated if it appears there is a positive change in the taxpayer's ability to pay which indicates collectability. See *IRM 5.16.1.2.9*. Usually this means your income has risen more than 20% from the previous year.
- All levies including those on Social Security and other government benefits will be released.
- Passports can be reissued when a case is in an *Installment Agreement* status or has been reported as *Currently Not Collectible* (CNC) status.
- Case Closing Letter 4223, Case Closed—*Currently Not Collectible*, will be issued to the taxpayer and/or Power of Attorney (POA) when a case is closed as CNC—hardship. *IRM 5.16.1.2.10 (04-13-2021)*

What is Economic Hardship to the IRS?

The levy/lien is creating an economic hardship due to the financial condition of an individual taxpayer. This condition applies if satisfaction of the levy in whole or in part will cause an individual taxpayer to be unable to pay his or her reasonable basic living expenses. The determination of a reasonable amount for basic living expenses will be made by the director and will vary according to the unique circumstances of the individual taxpayer. Unique circumstances, however, do not include the maintenance of an affluent or luxurious standard of living. Here is where *Form 433A and 433B* is vital to the taxpayer

Information from Taxpayer

In determining a reasonable amount for basic living expenses the director will consider any information provided by the taxpayer including:

- The taxpayer's age, employment status and history, ability to earn, number of dependents, or status as a dependent of someone else
- An amount reasonably necessary for food, clothing, housing (including utilities, home-owner insurance, home-owner dues, and the like), medical expenses (including health insurance), transportation, current tax payments (including federal, state, and local), alimony, child support, or other court-ordered payments, and expenses necessary to the taxpayer's production of income (such as dues for a trade union or professional organization, or child care payments which allow the taxpayer to be gainfully employed)
- The cost of living in the geographic area in which the taxpayer resides
- Any extraordinary circumstances such as special education expenses, a medical catastrophe, or natural disaster
- Any other factor that the taxpayer claims regarding economic hardship and brings this information to the attention of the IRS.
- There is a good faith requirement. In addition, in order to obtain a release of a levy, the taxpayer must act in good faith. Examples of failure to act in good faith include, but are not limited to, falsifying financial information, inflating actual expenses or costs, or failing to make full disclosure of assets.

You, the taxpayer, need to understand the terms. The reason is that the IRS wants two things from you. They want you to get current with filing all tax returns that should be filed and secondly, they want you to keep filing and paying taxes year after year into the

Chapter 11: Currently Not Collectible—When You Cannot Pay Your Back Taxes...

future. At the same time, they also want to get money for the back taxes. When you show them that you are not financially viable, and they look at your projected future income situation, they might see that you will be more likely to go from bad to worse rather than the other way around. So, your poverty may actually have meaning and value in negotiating with the IRS. Sometimes, in addition to declaring your case as *Currently not Collectible*, the IRS employee will also suggest that you should file an *Offer in Compromise* to settle the debt forever.

Here is a policy statement directly from the *Internal Revenue Manual*:

Policy Statement 5-71, Reporting accounts receivable as Currently not Collectible (CNC)— General

If, after taking all steps in the collection process, (IRM 5.15.1, Financial Analysis Handbook) it is determined that an account receivable is currently not collectible due to financial hardship, it should be so reported in order to remove it from active inventory.

- A hardship exists if a taxpayer is unable to pay reasonable basic living expenses.

- The basis for a hardship determination is from information about the taxpayer's financial condition provided on Form 433–A, Collection Information Statement for Wage Earners and Self-Employed Individuals or Form 433–B, Collection Information Statement for Businesses.

- Generally, these cases involve no income or assets, no equity in assets or insufficient income to make any payment without causing hardship.

- An account should not be reported as CNC if the taxpayer has income or equity in assets, and enforced collection of the income or assets would not cause hardship.

- However, if there are limited assets or income but it is determined that levy action would create a hardship, the liability may be reported as currently not collectible. A hardship exists if the levy action prevents the taxpayer from meeting necessary living expenses. In each case a determination must be made as to whether the levy would result in actual hardship, as distinguished from mere inconvenience to pay.

To reiterate, know your finances. Have your documentation. Speak to a tax professional if you are confused. This will save you your mental and financial health.

CHAPTER 12
IRS PENALTIES AND INTEREST

Penalty assessment is big business at the IRS. The IRS even admits it. The IRS has 140 penalties which are subjective and punitive as a deterrent to stop behaviors it does not like, such as filing and paying taxes late. The IRS charged taxpayer's $36 billion dollars in penalties in 2019. Sometimes as much as 60% to 80% of your balance due is made up of penalties. There is even a penalty called *failure to pay* that they charge to taxpayers who are actually paying on an *Installment Agreement*. If you make no payments on your tax due, you can expect penalties and interest to double the amount due in approximately eight years.

In your dealings with the IRS, it is likely that you will feel like you are just getting punished over and over. The balances continue to grow, and you are unable to fully pay or borrow the money, and you just keep getting more penalties and interest. Many taxpayers despair, and some lose hope that their tax balances will ever get paid.

The IRS Manual claims that: Penalties are to encourage voluntary compliance. Penalties should do the following:

- Be severe enough to deter noncompliance,
- Encourage noncompliant taxpayers to comply,
- Be objectively portioned to the offense, and
- Be used to educate taxpayers and encourage future compliance.

The penalties are supposed to be applied *fairly, consistently, and accurately.*

In 2016, Jim was asked by his company to move from Phoenix to Indianapolis. He chose not to. So, his company let him withdraw his pension contributions of $100,000. He used that to live for the next two years. But when he went to his tax preparer to file his tax return in 2017, he found out this pension distribution was taxable! So, Jim owed the IRS $40,000. Unfortunately, Jim only had $10,000 in tax withheld. Jim ultimately owed $30,000. Over three years, Jim paid $15,000 to the IRS. But the IRS tacked on $12,500 in penalties and interest, and they continue to add more every day. He still owes $27,500. Jim is a victim of Congress' law that the IRS enforces, where Jim was levied penalties and interest. Jim felt these added penalties and interests were punitive because he could never pay back the tax money owed. Jim's situation could be compared to a "Pay-Day Loan" situation. Jim's despair at the situation caused severe depression, and a citizen who was valuable to a society was now a burden.

For taxpayers seeking to comply with the tax laws, penalties are not intended to be a punishment. The IRS goal is to get the delinquent taxpayer back on the tax rolls and know that they will "voluntarily" file and pay in future years.

Many IRS employees tell taxpayers that penalties cannot be removed. In fact, some IRS employees are not even aware that these penalties are routinely removed. The IRS removes millions of dollars in penalties every day!

The IRS Manual (IRM) states that the IRS employee that you are working with may educate taxpayers and encourage future compliance by explaining the penalty, discussing the causes of your delinquency and listening to the reasons for noncompliance (IRM 20.1.1.2). IRS employees should be alert to information received in discussions with you that indicate possible reasons for the removal of penalties.

Sometimes the IRS will waive estimated tax penalties if the amount of tax due is under $1,000, where there was no tax liability the previous year, or the taxpayer is disabled or newly retired. This is found in the Internal Revenue Code Sec. 6654 (e).

Congress provides for penalties to be applied, and the IRS chooses to be very harsh in their application. The IRS has the authority to remove or abate penalties; they just don't like to do so until persuaded with valid reasons, such as IRC Section 7508 that states, "No penalties will be assessed against a taxpayer who is serving in a combat zone."

What You Need to Know to Get Penalties Removed

Types of Penalty Relief:
- *First Time Penalty Abatement.*
- *Reasonable Cause.*
- *Administrative Waiver* (The IRS chooses to remove penalties).
- *Statutory Exception* (A law giving this right to remove penalties).

First Time Penalty Abatement Waiver:
- Failure to file a tax return on time.
- Failing to pay your taxes on time.
- Failing to deposit taxes as required.

All other penalties can be abated or removed under the **Reasonable Cause** criteria.

What is Reasonable Cause, and How Do I Get It?

This is your chance to tell "your story" to the IRS, in a certified letter, explaining exactly what was happening in your life that contributed to missing the filing / paying deadlines.

You need to explain that you wanted to take care of your tax obligations, but due to circumstances or events beyond your control, you were unable to meet the tax requirement that caused the penalty to be applied. The following examples of circumstances that would raise the reasonable cause arguments may include things that happened in your life also.

Reasonable Cause Arguments for Individuals and Businesses

- You turned your records over to a tax professional, CPA, or to tax lawyers, and they lost or destroyed them or refused to return them to you.

- You were affected by a fire, flood, theft, casualty, or other natural disaster.

- You were in a terrorist situation or a war zone and were unable to meet your tax obligations.

- You acted in good faith to make sure that you were following the law and things happened that prevented you from doing so, such as you or a member of your family died, had a serious illness, or you were unavoidably absent from your residence because you had to care for another person. Also, the date and the length of time you were absent is important.

- Covid-19 could be a contributing factor for many Americans in not filing taxes in a timely manner.

- If you were out of the United States and unable to take care of your tax obligations.

- Despite your best efforts, you were unable to obtain the records needed to file your return or support an audit.

- You relied on the advice of a tax professional, CPA, or lawyer, and it proved to be wrong. However, you cannot blame another for failing to file your returns; i it is always your responsibility.

- Ignorant of the law. This can be claimed due to your mental state, level of education, or medical, emotional, and mental problems that affected you.

- A claim of *undue financial hardship* could cause the abatement of the failure

- to pay a penalty. Inability to pay, claiming lack of funds does not apply. The taxpayer must have had enough funds on hand, but as a result of unanticipated events, was unable to pay the taxes. Perhaps you were robbed, or you invested your tax money with a scam artist, a failing business, or experienced embezzlement by an employee. We have handled cases like this.

What is Your Story?

Remember what was happening in your life or your business that caused your IRS problems. This is not a blame game; it is seeking to tell your story truthfully because you may have what the IRS calls reasonable cause for the abating the penalties. In order for you to have penalties abated under the *Reasonable Cause* criteria, you must have *exercised ordinary business care and prudence* to take care of your tax obligations, but due to circumstances or events beyond your control, you were unable to meet the tax requirement that caused the penalty to be applied.

First, you must get your story together. Every taxpayer has a story about why they failed to file or pay their taxes. Your story can save you money. Let's go back to the beginning of your tax issue with the IRS. What was the primary triggering event that caused you not to file or pay your taxes or respond to the IRS? As so often happens, it is not usually just one thing that happened that caused your tax woes. Even though there might have been a triggering event, other complications compounded that event and continued long after the actual situation. This can cover many areas.

The IRS will look at your filing history and see if you have had any problems in the last three years with filing or paying. This is not a stand-alone factor, just something that they keep in mind. If you have filed and paid on time, that is a plus for you.

Secondly, they will consider the length of time between the event cited as a reason for non-compliance combined with when you finally did file your tax return or when you tried to correct the situation.

An example of this would be if a few months before your tax

return was due, a member of your family died. In the time after the death, you may have been in mourning or had to move, take care of an elderly parent, change jobs, or whatever other event that death caused in your life. All that change might have caused you to become depressed or use drugs or alcohol to self-medicate, and then you missed work. That could change the focus to make the case qualify for penalty abatement. But if you did not file your tax return until two years later, then they would deny it on those grounds. Remember, and this is the important idea in this chapter, nothing stands alone.

There usually are many factors involved in every transaction in life. The IRS employee is not a mind reader. You must give the IRS all of the facts and circumstances to present your case for *reasonable cause* for the abatement of penalties. Tell them everything! IRS employees, especially field employees such as *Revenue Officers* and *Revenue Agents*, are trained to ask tough questions to see if your story is consistent with other known facts. Be prepared for follow-up questions that might be asked of you.

Here's another example. Someone else had control of your tax records—an accountant or bankruptcy trustee or some other third party—so that is why you could not file on time. That is an acceptable reason, as long as you can show you attempted to get those records returned. The IRS will look at how long it took for you to file after you finally got the records back. Again, there are often other circumstances that might have occurred at the same time, such as you were in divorce proceedings, depressed, had lost your job, or other factors.

Perhaps you did not file a return or make tax payments in the time required, or you claimed credits, exemptions, and deductions on your tax return, and now you don't have the receipts to prove those deductions to the IRS. Maybe you never had them. At this point, it does not matter.

What matters is what you were thinking at the time that you made the decision to not file or pay or do whatever else the IRS is applying the penalty for. This is what the IRS calls "your intent." What did you intend to do at the time? Those are the facts of your case.

How to Write Your Penalty Appeal Letter

The letter should be addressed to whatever office sent you the most recent letter. You must include your name, address, Social Security number, and then you should state that you are protesting the penalties and interest on your case because you have either *Reasonable Cause for Penalty Abatement* or are requesting the abatement under *First Time Penalty Abatement Waiver (FTAW)*. You have to ask for this to happen. The IRS could automatically apply this waiver, but it does not. The *Inspector General for Tax Administration (TIGTA)* reported that in 2012, 1.65 million individual taxpayers qualified for FTAW, but only 145,200 (8.8%) asked for it. This is because most taxpayers and even some tax representatives do not know about this valuable tool. If the IRS employee working your case refuses to take this penalty away, ask that your case be referred to the *Office of Appeals* then follow up with that request in writing.

The IRS has the power to take away penalties but is very reluctant to do so. However, if you don't ask for penalty abatement, then the answer is always "No!" Do not be afraid; this is not difficult. See the sample letters to send to the IRS at the end of this chapter. Sample letters are also available as PDF files at TaxReliefforYou.com and RichardSchickel.com.

What the IRS Looks for When It Reviews Your Protest Letter

IRS employees are allowed but not encouraged to abate penalties, even though they are authorized to do so in the Internal Revenue Manual *(IRM)*. They will always look for something that they think you did wrong and use this action as a reason to deny your request to abate the penalties. Additionally, you have to ask for penalty relief—it will not be just offered to you.

Audit/Examination Penalties

Tens of billions of dollars in penalties are manually assessed every year by the Examination/ Audit Division.

Accuracy-Related Penalty (IRC 6662) types can be found in IRM 20.1.5.1.6.1. The most common penalties are the *Accura-*

cy-Related penalties. This penalty accounts for 20% to 40% of the tax that the IRS is claiming you underpaid. Assessment of *Accuracy-Related Penalties* by the IRS is up 800% for the period 2005-2010. If you feel the IRS employee has not explained it adequately for your understanding, you should ask to speak to their supervisor.

The *Accuracy-Related Penalty* is assessed if you overstate your deductions and expenses. There are many reasons for this penalty. This penalty is on top of the normal *Failure to File and Pay penalties*, and interest is also charged on the penalty and the tax deficiency. The second penalty is the *Civil Fraud Penalty* which is 75% of your new tax amount. Note that this is different from the *Criminal Fraud Penalty*, which comes with criminal cases. The *Criminal Fraud Penalty* is $100,000 and a maximum five-year prison term.

Generally, taxpayers are not subject to the *Accuracy-Related Penalty* if they establish that they had reasonable cause for the underpayment and acted in good faith. The most important factor is that the taxpayer made an effort to determine and present the correct tax return to the IRS. The burden of proof for establishing reasonable cause is on the taxpayer. In other words—you have to ask for it and prove why you deserve it.

Your best defense in these cases is to appeal the penalties to the IRS agent, and then if you are unsuccessful, appeal to their immediate manager. In my experience, this will usually involve admitting to part or all of their proposed tax additions to you. It also makes the case easier for the IRS to process if you agree to sign the *Revenue Agent Report (RAR)* or *Consent Form* to allow the agent to assess the additional tax. This puts them in a better mood because they know that you will not go to the *Office of Appeals* or Tax Court to dispute the tax amount, which costs the government a whole lot of money for the IRS to have to prove their case against you all over again.

This is true if you have been caught in not reporting income or you have no documentation to support your deductions and expense claims. If the IRS agent and their manager refuse to discuss or negotiate the penalties, then you can file a request to go to *Appeals*, where there is a much higher probability that some or all of these penalties will be removed.

The IRS looks at your compliance history, i.e., was this just a slip-up in one or two years only? Did you maintain adequate books and records and take actions to ensure that the tax reported was correct? You must present your story about what happened and why it happened in order to have a greater chance of success with penalty abatement.

Again, and this is important, I have seen cases where the IRS will not assess as many penalties if the taxpayer signs that they agree to the audit increase. This is in the best interests of both the IRS and the taxpayer. Because then the IRS knows the case will not later go to *Appeals* or Tax Court.

IRS Computer Will Sting You

The *Automated Under-Reporter System* (AUR) is a computer program that matches information reported to the IRS by various sources required to report to it. For example, the *Form 1099* is sent by businesses to the IRS. No human being looks at your case. It matches that information to your return. It will automatically assess penalties if your tax return meets its selection criteria. Penalties are automatically assessed without any review by an IRS employee and assessed without the Penalty's managerial approval. The computer solely does this action.

The First Line of Appeal

The IRS *Examination/Audit Employees* must have their managers' approval to assess any penalties, thus, the manager is your first line of appeal. The burden of proof to establish the Penalty is on the IRS. Then the burden of proof shifts to you to establish why the penalty should not be assessed, such as reasonable cause. You can always pay the tax in full (including the Penalty) and file a timely claim for a refund which becomes a refund suit in the US District Court of Federal Claims. If your case looks like it is heading in that direction, then you need a tax attorney.

I had one case where the proposed new tax was $2 million, and the fraud and accuracy penalties were $500,000, and I persuaded the IRS to waive the penalties in full because the taxpayer consented to the new higher tax amount.

Businesses Have a Higher Standard Expected of Them

When you are in business, you must show that you *exercised ordinary business care and prudence*. This means you operated your business with a profit motive, that you kept good books and records, and that you supervised every aspect of your business, including monitoring what your employees were doing.

Examples of not being in control of your business are saying that you do not like to do the books or issue checks, so you have a signature stamp made, and then an employee authorizes checks and embezzles money from your company.

Being short of money because a customer filed bankruptcy or failed to pay their bill is not reasonable cause.

Could the company have anticipated what happened? Should they have reduced payroll or increased workload in order to make sure that taxes were being paid that they were able to pay? If so, the request for reasonable cause will likely be denied.

The IRS looks at the last three years of tax compliance; if you had that same Penalty in the past, you are unlikely to get it abated now.

The IRS Will Remove Huge Business Penalties

Over the years, IRS employees have discovered many cases of embezzlement that occurred in businesses and involved federal taxes. One case that was noteworthy involved a doctor who was very successful, bringing home $500,000 a year in income. He grew old and decided to sell his practice, so outside accountants came in and conducted a due diligence audit. They looked at his books and records going back seven years. They discovered that his office manager/bookkeeper had been embezzling for that whole time. He trusted her completely as they had known each other since high school and went to the same church.

Somewhere along the way, she became jealous of his lifestyle and resented the fact that he only paid her $42,000 a year. At first, she started slowly embezzling money to fund shopping and vacation trips. That should have been a signal, but the doctor never noticed. About two years into the theft, an outside CPA conducted an audit and discovered that about $240,000 was missing. For some reason, instead of telling the doctor directly, he discussed it extensively over drinks with the office manager/bookkeeper, and well, one thing led to another; they started having an affair and stealing the money together.

How this relates to the taxes is that the doctor's employees had money taken out of their paychecks for income and Social Security taxes (the Trust Fund Taxes are included here), but the office manager never paid the money to the IRS. This happened in the last three years of the crime. That is how the balance grew so rapidly. Then the IRS came and told the doctor that he owed $1.7 million, and about $700,000 was just penalties.

The *IRS Revenue Officer* reviewed what happened, plugged the facts into the *Reasonable Cause Assistant Calculator*, and it rejected the claim for *penalty abatement* because the embezzlement had gone over six months without discovery.

But the *Revenue Officer* did not feel right about that decision, so he chose to override it manually. The IRS decided that if the doctor would file criminal charges against the former office manager, they would abate $700,000 in penalties because he had conducted his business in a manner that was professional and exercised *ordinary business care and prudence in operating the company.*

The fact that he had relied on professionals to do his accounting and audits helped. The office manager was sentenced to four years' probation after she claimed that she had a drinking and gambling problem, and the CPA lost everything. The bookkeeper was mostly unemployable after that and never paid one dime in restitution.

The IRS Rarely Removes These Types of Penalties

The IRS never removes the bad check penalty.

Penalty abatement for abusive transactions, frivolous returns, *Accuracy-Related Penalty*, civil and criminal fraud, negligence, and other abusive conduct are usually very difficult to remove but not impossible. This is because the IRS will be judging you on many different levels to determine if you are truly reformed from this behavior and attitudes. They will also look at your behavior if you are prominent in anti-government or anti-IRS groups, now or in the past. The IRS looks at what would the public perception be if the penalty were abated. For instance, a CPA or tax preparer who has been filing returns and seeking fraudulent tax refunds for himself or his clients would not stand a chance of getting penalties abated. The same story applies to an activist who uses anti-IRS rhetoric.

Businesses pay income, employment, and excise taxes. They are held to a higher standard that the IRS uses to determine if they are making an effort to comply with the tax laws.

Does the IRS Ever Remove Interest?

The IRS will tell you that interest can never be abated, but that is not true. There are IRS employees who are known as *Interest Abatement Coordinators* who will make the final in-IRS decision if the IRS abates interest. *Appeals* and *Tax Court* have this authority also.

Interest can be removed when:

- The IRS makes an error such as in a processing or math error.
- When the IRS is responsible for unreasonable delays in processing, such as when the IRS fails to contact the taxpayer within three years of the tax return filing in question and then begins an audit. (See IRM 20.2.7.4)
- When the tax is found not legally to be due.
- Interest is also suspended when members of the military are in combat zones or under military deferment.
- Interest can be suspended or not assessed for taxpayers in a declared disaster area due to weather-related disaster, terrorist or military action.
- When you are in bankruptcy, interest is suspended and sometimes is canceled by the bankruptcy court.
- When an erroneous refund is issued due to no fault of the taxpayer, and it is under $50,000.

- The IRS under IRC 6404 (a) and as explained in IRM 20.2.7.2, can abate interest that is:
- Excessive in amount,
- Assessed after the statutory period of limitations has expired, or
- Erroneously or illegally assessed.

With each of these arguments, the IRS will automatically fight you but don't give up. If you believe that you have cause, you should always request that interest be also abated.

Interest Abatement is Never Granted Solely Because of Reasonable Cause.

Interest abatement must fit the very strict and limited circumstances that you and your tax professional can find in the Internal Revenue Code.

Taxpayer Advocate Service

The second line of defense is to contact the *Taxpayer Advocate Service* (www.irs.gov/Advocate) because trying to figure out what to do to defend yourself against IRS penalties and interest is very confusing. This is an agency outside of the IRS. Some taxpayers have difficulty understanding their rights or obtaining a solution to a problem. This avenue is open to you when you have made or attempted to make two or more contacts where the IRS system or individual employees were not responsive, and the IRS could not resolve your case by the date promised.

Sample Letters to Apply for Penalty Abatement (Removal)

Two penalty abatement boilerplate letters are provided. This information is printed here and available online, where it can be copied and pasted into your computer. Then, you can input your information, tell your story, sign it, and mail it (certified) to the address on the last IRS letter you have received. This applies to all *Individual Income Tax Returns (Form 1040)* and all business tax returns, including *Form 1120/the 1120S, (Corporate Income Tax), Form 1065(Partnership Tax Return), Form 940 (Federal Unemployment Tax),* and *Form 941 (Employers Quarterly Tax Return).*

First Time Penalty Abatement Request Letter

To: Internal Revenue Service

Address: (Address on last IRS letter you received)

From: (Your Full Name(s) and Full Address)

(Social Security Number(s) or Employer Identification Number)

Re: First-time Penalty Abatement Waiver Letter (Insert Letter Number CP or LT or LTR. Found on the upper right corner of the latest IRS letter that you received.)

Date: (The date you are sending the letter)

Tax Year: (The tax year(s) you are writing about)

I request a First-time Penalty Abatement for my Individual Income Tax return for the year ended December 31, 20___ based on my compliance history. This request applies to any Failure to File, Failure to Pay, or Failure to Deposit penalties. I have filed and paid my current year's taxes and my previous three years' tax returns. I request this under the Internal Revenue Manual Section 20.1.1.3.3.2.1 and IRM 20.1.1.3.6.1.1A.

If this abatement is denied, I request penalty abatement under the Reasonable Cause provisions of the Internal Revenue Manual 20.1.2.2.4.1. And IRM 20-1.1.3.2.2.2.

I had issues that prevented me from filing timely in this year-Covid-19, *unemployment, physical or mental health problems, or explain additional reasons here-*

I request a manual review of this case because the Reasonable Cause Assistant cannot process the specific circumstances of my case.

Please process this request; I seek to resolve the tax and penalty portions that remain after penalty abatement separately, based on my circumstances.

If you reject my penalty abatement request, I request that this case be sent to the Office of Appeals.

(SIGN YOUR NAME)

Chapter 12: IRS Penalties & Interest

Reasonable Cause Abatement of Penalties Letter

To: Internal Revenue Service

Address: (Address on last IRS letter you received)

From: (Your Full Name(s) and Full Address)

(Social Security Number(s) or Employer Identification Number)

Re: Letter for Reasonable Cause Abatement of Penalties

Date: (Date sending letter)

Regarding: Letter number (Insert *CP or LT or LTR* found on the upper right corner of the latest IRS letter that you receive.)

I request that all penalties and interest be abated from my tax account for (INCOME TAX, OR EMPLOYMENT TAXES) the periods and years listed here. For example, Form 1040 for the year ended 12-31-2020. I request this under the reasonable cause provisions of the Internal Revenue Manual (IRM 20.1.2.2.4.1. And IRM 20-1.1.3.2.2.2.)

I exercised ordinary business care and prudence in determining my tax obligation. I acted in good faith. I did not willfully neglect my duty to comply with the tax laws because of the following: (any that apply)

- Due to Covid-19
- Due to Covid-19 related circumstances
- Due to natural disasters, floods, hurricanes, earthquakes, or tornados.
- Due to military or terrorist action that affected me
- Due to illness or injury to my family or people close to me
- Due to the destruction of records
- Due to negligence by tax preparers/tax professionals
- Due to an error by the IRS or advice given by an IRS employee
- Due to hospitalizations required because of accidents, injuries, or death of family or people close to me.
- Due to loss of records or records not obtainable by me
- Due to the loss of my job or my spouse's job
- Due to the death of a family member or person close to me
- Due to business closing due to Covid

- Due to business permanently closing, bankruptcy, or other financial disasters
- Due to divorce
- Due to alcohol/drug abuse issues
- Due to drug abuse (legal or illegal)
- Due to mental issues, including Covid-19, depression, bi-polar or other
- Due to physical abuse, sexual abuse, mental abuse, or emotional abuse
- Due to sexual addiction
- Due to gambling addiction
- Due to other circumstances affecting me, my family, or those I am close to.
- Due to fire
- Due to burglary, theft of records needed to prepare my return
- Due to being out of the country for military or business reasons for (state how long)

I request a manual review of this case because the Reasonable Cause Assistant cannot process the specific circumstances of my case.

Please process this request; I seek to resolve the tax and penalty portions that remain after penalty abatement separately, based on my circumstances.

If you reject my penalty abatement request, I request that this case be sent to the Office of Appeals.

Again, I request that my case be reviewed manually.

(SIGN YOUR NAME)

CHAPTER 13

WHEN DO YOU NEED TO PREPARE FORM 433–A/B FINANCIAL STATEMENTS?

Is the IRS asking for a Financial Statement? This chapter is to instruct you on how to prepare a financial statement if your case is assigned to a *Revenue Officer* or if you are unable to pay your taxes now or in the future. Remember that *Revenue Officers* cannot presently offer you the Secret New IRS agreement for amounts under $250,000. They still do it the old-fashioned way of requesting financial statements and then reviewing them to decide what you should pay in your agreement. (Also, see Supplement B for more instructions on this topic.)

The Secret to Preparing IRS Financial Statements

Recent changes in the deals that IRS is offering are: the IRS will request a *Form 433-A Collection Information Statement for Individuals* or a *Form 433-B Collection Information Statement for Businesses* in all circumstances when you are working with a *Revenue Officer*. **Never** use *Form 433-F Collection Information Statement*. The need for a financial statement is disjointed and can harm good, honest people who are simply trying to get an *Installment Agreement*.

For *Installment Agreements*

The IRS's attitude to the taxpayer is of always wanting delinquent taxpayers to pay their taxes right now or as quickly as possible, no matter what. This is usually without regard for the taxpayer's current employment situation, physical and mental health, or income and expenses. The IRS just wants its money.

Many delinquent taxpayers call the IRS and want to "do the right thing" and agree to pay their tax balances over time. These taxpayers are ill-prepared for the aggressive IRS collection interview techniques. The IRS will ask rapid-fire questions designed to get as much financial information out of delinquent taxpayers as fast as they can to get them into an *Installment Agreement* (IA). This aggressive technique creates problems because it forces taxpayers to make IA's that they cannot afford. Thus, this policy leads to high default rates for IRS IA's of at least 28% to 78%.

Did you know that the law requires the IRS to stop and listen to the taxpayer's situation before setting the terms of an *Installment Agreement*?

The secret to gaining the best advantage for your case to always claim the maximum allowed expenses on the *Collection Information Statement* (CIS), not some lesser amount.

The *Collection Information Statements* (CIS) (*Form 433-A*) and (*Form 433-B*) are the best tools available for you to present your complete financial picture to the IRS. The IRS lives by numbers and laws, so use those numbers to support your case goals. **Never use** *Form 433-F, Collection Information Statement,* because it does not offer all of the rights due to the taxpayer. A study of (Internal Revenue Manual) IRM 5.15 explains in detail how IRS employees are supposed to review CIS forms.

Google *IRS Allowable Expenses* and it will tell you exactly the amounts that the IRS will allow you in the area where you live. It will cover food, housing, health expenses, and automobile ownership, and operating expenses.

What you may be allowed for your living expenses may seem like too little money to support your current lifestyle. The IRS does not care about that. The IRS policy is that when you decided not to

Chapter 13: When Do You Need to Prepare Form 433-A/B Financial Statement?

pay your taxes, you gave up some of your rights. For example, the IRS will not allow you to pay credit card payments, donations to church or charities, unsecured debt, or other expenses that may be a normal part of your life.

So, I think that you need to be honest about your expenses. For instance, pet care is generally not allowed as an expense, but I have seen emotional support animal expenses allowed.

The IRS does not allow luxury cars, boats, second homes, campers, Quads, jet skis, jewelry, fur coats, or items purchased at a luxury store you don't need for daily living. Luxury cars include Mercedes, BMW, Lexus, Porsche—you get the idea. If you have a business need for a flashy car, claim it and see what they allow. This may apply to realtors and business owners.

The *Internal Revenue Code Section 7122* (the Law) states that **"IRS employees shall not use the *Allowable Expenses* to the extent that such use would result in the taxpayer not having adequate means to provide for basic living expenses."** This section mandates that the IRS "develop and publish schedules of national and local allowances designed to provide taxpayer's entering into an *Installment Agreement*, *Offer in Compromise* or a *Currently Not collectible* situation. (IA) have an adequate means to provide for basic living expenses".

With respect to *Installment Agreements*, the Internal Revenue Manual 5.15.1 (IRM) provides: "Guidelines are designed to account for basic living expenses. In some cases, based on a taxpayer's individual facts and circumstances, it may be appropriate to deviate from the standard amount when failure to do so will cause the taxpayer economic hardship".

One right that was not available before 1998 is the implementation of the National and Local IRS *Allowable Expenses*. The *Allowable Living Expense (ALE) Standards* a/k/a as *Collection Financial Standards (CFS)* provides for a minimum standard of living to apply to every taxpayer, to cover food, clothing, housekeeping, housing, utilities, auto ownership, and auto operating expenses plus out of pocket health care expenses.

If an amount is claimed by the taxpayer which exceeds the standard (ALE), then the taxpayer must provide reasonable substantiation and documentation. If you research the ALE, you will notice that the IRS allowances are not enough to cover actual living expenses.

Taxpayers should make written communications in responding to the IRS on *Form 9465* or *Form 433-D*. This format offers ample opportunity to present your request for an *Installment Agreement* (IA) with more reasonable terms.

There is no place on the *Collection Information Statement (CIS)* forms to explain your circumstances; this leads to taxpayers committing to IA's that they cannot afford. So, attach a sheet of paper with your story and mail it via certified letter explaining what is going on in your life, job-wise, physical, and mental health-wise. It is completely confidential and will never be shared by IRS.

It is very important to document any mental or physical health issues that affect you or your family. How? If you have a medical history online you can download your doctor visits with your doctor's summaries and prescriptions. Attach a statement with the taxpayer's age and prior conditions (drug, alcohol, or gambling addiction) and other existing conditions to explain why the health insurance usage is anticipated to be higher than other taxpayers.

Jim worked at a construction site and fell and hurt his back when he was fifty years old. This injury required him to be off work for six months because of back surgery and rehabilitation. In filling out his CIS, Jim sent the IRS the *Forms 433A/B* with a certified letter and his downloaded medical doctor summaries from My Chart. This documentation gave credulity to his health issues that are ongoing and revealed a special circumstance. The IRS deferred collection on his account and close his case as *Currently Not Collectible Due to Financial Hardship*.

How to Present Income Earned

- When presenting your income, only include the base income. Do not include bonuses, overtime, and variable shift differential pay unless they are fixed and regularly occurring.

- If you are presenting self-employed income, make sure to reduce it by deducting whatever the amount of expenses, for example, transportation, marketing, supplies, postage, office, and professional fees.
- If your business has income from procuring some product, make sure to include the cost of goods sold information as an expense. The IRS usually accepts whatever is listed as income from your Schedule C, LLC, or Subchapter S corporation or partnership return. They hardly ever question any of the expenses. They never question the cost of goods sold. In fact, partnership tax returns are so complex that very few agents even work such cases.

Income of Non-Liable Spouses, Roommates, and Dependents

Prior to the current tax law, you may have had dependents or family and friends who lived with you and claimed them as dependents; this is no longer available. Since the *Allowable Expenses* may give a taxpayer more money for extra people living in their house, you may be tempted to claim them on the financial statement as well. *This will inflate your expenses,* and IRS will try to include all or part of their income with the taxpayers. This increases your income, and IRS comes up with a higher *Installment Agreement* than the taxpayer can reasonably afford.

If you are in this situation, you may have to list elderly or disabled relatives with their own Social Security or Disability Income on your *Collection Information Statements (CIS)*. Then list all of *their* expenses, so there is no net gain to the you.

First of all, a delinquent taxpayer should never be on a "bank account" with their dependents and should not be the "representative payee" for anyone's Social Security benefits. The IRS could issue a levy, and the non-liable person's money could be taken as well. If the delinquent taxpayer provides financial services and support for their claimed dependents (elderly/disabled), they should be the representative payee.

If the IRS insists that a percentage of the dependent's income be reported to be included as a percentage of the delinquent taxpayer's income on the CIS, try to expense out the food, gas, food, goods, and services of their dependent. Thus, the delinquent taxpayer can include that percent on their CIS.

Be sure to include all other related expenses such as caregiver, respite, special diet, transportation, and whatever else they choose to spend their own money on.

Be careful with this type of disclosure. The IRS will question you about these expenses trying to discover your dependent's income and then include that income on the taxpayer's financial statement. If IRS determines that a dependent pay rent of, say, $500 a month to the taxpayer, the IRS will want that included on the taxpayer's CIS and sometimes insist that it be reported on the individual's income tax return.

Although the assets and income of a non-liable person may be reviewed to determine the taxpayer's portion of the shared household income and expenses, they are generally not included when calculating the amount, the taxpayer can pay. One notable exception is community property states. Follow the community property laws in these states to determine what assets and income of the otherwise non-liable spouse are subject to tax collection. If you are confused or have any questions, contact a tax professional.

How the IRS Reviews Collection Information Statements

All IRS collection employees reviewing financial statements can ask for additional documentation. Usually, this is limited to three months of bank statements. Here's a tip, your tax professionals should always meticulously review those bank statements for any other income or expenses before they are sent on to the IRS.

The IRS may also request copies of other monthly expenses. These may include pay stubs, proof of housing and utility expenses, car payments, child care, child support, out-of-pocket medical expenses that exceed the allowed amount, and copies of agreements to pay past-due State and local taxes that you might owe.

The IRS evaluates financial statements using the collection standards. Total allowable expenses are defined as "expenses that meet the necessary expense test"—expenses that are necessary to provide for a taxpayer's and their family's health and welfare and/or production of income. The expenses must be reasonable. The IRS states in this document (IRM 5.15.1.2.4.16) that "the current standards fail to provide adequate expenses for taxpayers residing in high-cost communities."

Many IRS collection employees fail to exercise discretion as allowed by the Internal Revenue Code (IRC) and the Internal Revenue Manual (IRM) when applying the standards. Employees in the *Automated Collection System (ACS)* are even less likely to be flexible than *Revenue Officers* when applying the standards. "The failure to exercise discretion" results in more defaulted *Installment Agreements* and reduces the number of accepted *Offer in Compromise's (OIC)*, and motivates taxpayers to seek bankruptcy relief from tax obligations. Some IRS employees are willing to work with the "taxpayer's unique issues," but many are not. This failure to exercise discretion loses money for the US government and continues the reputation of negativity for the IRS.

Some expense amounts are provided automatically, whether the taxpayer spends that much or not. These are food, public transportation or automobile operating expenses, and out-of-pocket health care expenses. These are allowed without questioning the amounts that they actually spend per IRM 5.15.1.7.3 (a) (b). Always put down the full *Allowable Living Standards Expense* (ALE) amount even if you do not spend that much money every month.

Make sure to look at your financial and life situation and plan for what can go wrong in dealing with the IRS. You may live in a place with higher expenses such as greater than normal commuting costs or other job-related expenses that you have to pay personally. Any expense that can be explained as reasonable and necessary for the production of income is an allowable expense.

Generally, the IRS will not argue with Court-Ordered Payments (alimony, child support, including by the state, and other court-ordered payments.) If alimony and child support payments are court-ordered and being paid, they are allowable. If payments are not being made, the IRS will do not allow the expense unless the non-payment was due to temporary job loss or illness. Restitution payments made to other victims pursuant to a court order are allowable expenses.

Food, Clothing, and Other Expenses—Allowable Living Standards (ALS)

Taxpayers get *Allowable Living Standards* (ALS) with regards to food, clothing, and other expenses in full, whether they spend that much money or not on these expenses. The IRS cannot disallow this amount, ever, because it is published on the ALS. Taxpayers need to know exactly how much the IRS allows for each expense category. This means the taxpayer must look up the expenses allowed for their area.

The Categories are:

- **Food**—This includes all food at home or away from home. If the taxpayer has a medical condition that calls for a special diet, such as gluten-free, vegan, allergy-related, organic, Keto, weight loss, diabetic-friendly diet, or medicines as prescribed by a doctor, then all expenses are normal and allowable expenses even if they exceed the amount already allowed by the ALS. $400 per person.

- **Housekeeping supplies**—This includes laundry, cleaning supplies, postage, lawn and garden supplies. $41 per person.

- **Apparel & services**—This includes clothing and footwear purchases and dry cleaning. A business professional might easily exceed this standard if they wear suits to work. If so, document that expense, and IRS should allow it because it is related to "production of income expense." This could include uniforms that the taxpayer has to wear in order to work, as well as safety equipment and safety shoes. $92 per person

- **Personal care products & services**—This includes products for the hair, oral hygiene products, shaving needs, and electrical personal care appliances. $42.

- **Miscellaneous**—The IRS states in its *National Standards* directions that taxpayers can use the miscellaneous allowance to pay for expenses such as credit card payments, bank fees and charges, reading material, and school supplies. It can also be used for private school tuition or tithing at church. $148 per person per month. No deviations from the miscellaneous allowance are allowed.

- All categories total $723 per person per month.

"If the IRS determines that the facts and circumstances of a taxpayer's situation indicate that using the (ALS) standards is inadequate to provide for basic living expenses, we may allow for actual expenses. However, taxpayers must provide documentation that supports a determination that using national and local expense standards leaves them with an inadequate means of providing for basic living expenses." (Source: *Collection Financial Standards*. IRM 5.15) (Google it.)

These allowed amounts do not come anywhere near the expected costs to live in the US today. I believe the ALS standards need to be changed to accurately reflect for all taxpayers a current minimum standard of living as required by the *Internal Revenue Code* (IRC). These standards need to be reviewed and increased yearly.

Housing Related Expenses—Local Standards— Housing and Utilities

The *Allowable Living Standards* rarely provide a realistic number that reflects what taxpayers could expect to spend each month for these expenses. This standard includes mortgage or rent, property taxes, interest, insurance, maintenance, repairs, gas, electric, water, sewer, heating oil, garbage collection, residential telephone service, and cell phone service, cable television, and internet service. This is an area where taxpayers often underestimate their expenses. For example, in the area of housing expenses, sometimes homeowners report what their mortgage amount is but forget they are paying real estate taxes separately. Thus, they forget to include these real estate taxes on their CIS. The IRS can allow for more expenses if the case is made that those expenses are higher.

Taxpayers have the right to live in a safe, habitable residence. The IRS cannot deny taxpayers these expenses as long as the taxpayer has adequate documentation of those expenses. Documentation is the critical piece. The IRS will argue for the local standard amount in most cases, but this can be appealed with visible receipts, bills, and payments.

Sometimes, a taxpayer will be required to live within so many miles or minutes of their job; this is common for hospital doctors and nurses. So, this may require them to live in a higher-cost housing market. The same can apply to taxpayers who are working split shifts or are required to live within the city where they are employed. This can be claimed if it is in your employment contract.

If you have sufficient equity in your home to pay your taxes fully, expect the IRS to direct you to try to borrow and get some equity out, or they may even threaten to seize the equity in the house. The IRS has that right. If that occurs, try to borrow from two lenders, and then when you are rejected for loans, you should ask for a rejection letter that can be supplied to the IRS. Taxpayers can apply for loans all day long, but without sufficient income to repay a loan, the IRS will not be able to force you to borrow on your home or sell your house.

Houses need repairs, and maintenance, just to retain their value. Houses have sudden and unexpected repairs and immediate maintenance that taxpayers have not budgeted for. For instance, this can include a new refrigerator, dishwasher, water heater, stove, furnace, air conditioner, plumbing, electrical repairs, sewer, irrigation systems, septic fields, and roof repairs. The taxpayer often uses their credit card to pay this unexpected expense, and the taxpayer under-reports these expenses to the IRS.

If the taxpayer uses a credit card to purchase any of the above items, then the IRS must allow the cost of that payment. Please note, your case may have to go to Appeals on that, but you will win.

Another area taxpayers underestimate is for the cost of their

Chapter 13: When Do You Need to Prepare Form 433-A/B Financial Statement?

utility service. For instance, in the cold northern United States, winter gas and oil bills can be hundreds of dollars a month in older homes. In warmer areas, air conditioning bills may swell in summer. Outside expenses like yard maintenance may be much higher for an ill or elderly taxpayer than for younger taxpayers. The city may have codes requiring lawn maintenance which is a liability to the taxpayer.

It is recommended that you list the full allowable expense in your home zip code and if it is significantly higher, then argue for its inclusion. The IRS is *automatically authorized* to accept a 5% deviation of the allowable expense number. A tax professional could argue for even more expenses if it can be proven that by not allowing the expense, it will damage the value of the home or affect the health, safety, and welfare of the taxpayer and their family.

Taxpayers may also own rental housing that, in some real estate markets, is impossible to sell because they are upside down on the investment. This means the taxpayer overpaid for their property and owes more than the house is currently worth. These taxpayers would actually have to bring $11,000 to $20,000 cash to a sale just to close the sale of their property. As long as the rental property is rented and not costing the taxpayer anything, the IRS will usually allow the property owner to keep the rental property. After all, the rental house would be covered as an asset that the IRS federal tax lien would attach to in the event of a sale.

Before the current more liberal *installment agreement* terms became available, the IRS would allow an expense like a rent payment or mortgage that exceeds the allowable expense amount. It can be allowed at a higher rate for one year, and then the taxpayer would have time to relocate to a place that is more reasonably priced or be forced to use other monies to pay the difference in payment that would be disallowed after the first year. This is known as the *One Year Rule* and the *Five-Year Rule*. Google these terms for more information; they only apply to a rare number of cases.

Automobile Related Expenses—Transportation

This includes public transportation or auto loans or lease payments, maintenance, repairs, insurance, fuel, registrations, licenses inspections, parking, and tolls. Some taxpayers have older vehicles that increasingly need more and more maintenance. For instance, replacing a transmission, head gasket, or suspension system can cost $3,000 or more. Because it has been reported that a majority of Americans live paycheck to paycheck. A $400 unexpected expense it is a hardship because they have no savings.

All of these life problems can come up suddenly, and this can cause a taxpayer to default their *IRS Installment Agreement (IA)* in order to pay the surprise expenses of daily living as listed previously.

IRS does allow taxpayers to claim $200 extra a month if the taxpayer's car is over eight years old or has more than 100,000 miles. This is a reasonable claim considering that older vehicles will require much more maintenance than a newer one. So, it is reasonable to argue for the inclusion of this expense with *Revenue Officers* and *Group Managers*. I have won the claim for $200 extra per month in *Appeals*.

Some expenses, such as a car payment, can be larger than allowed because the vehicle is used in business for the production of income. Realtors would argue that they need cars that make them look successful in order to attract clients. The IRS does not look kindly on taxpayers who are driving luxury automobiles. Again, examples of luxury cars would be Lexus, Infinity, Mercedes, etc. Don't expect the IRS to allow those extra costs for vehicles like that.

- Some taxpayers may have higher than usual commuting expenses. In this case, they may drive to a paid parking lot to catch a commuter train and then, when they get to the city, take a subway train to their workplace.
- Workers who use their vehicles to drive from job to job or have higher than usual commuting expenses all qualify for an exemption to the rules. An example would be a salesman, truck driver, or "floater" for a company.

- It is essential for taxpayers to be able to get to work. All taxpayers should purchase a new car or recently used car and an extended warranty for an amount that the ALS allows for their location.

Insurance Payments

Life and health insurance are usually allowed. As long as the amount of life insurance is deemed appropriate based on the taxpayer's age, health, and lifestyle, and his dependents, it is an expense. However, this could be debated at length with a *Revenue Officer* or *Appeals Officer*.

Health insurance is an expense that taxpayers often underreport. The IRS employees who have great health insurance do not understand private health insurance issues and its costs and deductibles. The taxpayer or his advocate must get the information to document the amount that will be required for out-of-pocket co-pays and deductibles. Out of pocket includes eyeglasses, contact lenses, medical services such as medical doctor visits and dental visits. Additionally, braces for children, special medical care required for children with medical problems such as autism, learning disabilities, respite care, etc., are out-of-pocket expenses. The taxpayer should get a prescription from their doctor or dentist showing that this expense is medically necessary, and then IRS is compelled to honor it.

For instance, the normal medical deductible for a single person is $5,000 a year. This amount should be divided over twelve months ($416 a month) and then be added to the deductibles along with the cost of the monthly policy. The monthly policy can be as high as $1300 per month, depending upon the medical history of the taxpayer. Taxpayers can expect an argument from the IRS regarding this deduction, but a prudent person would budget their income to address all foreseeable health expenses.

Other Expenses

- The IRS does not allow anything for savings or emergencies. It does not allow for 401k or other retirement savings. It usually does not allow anything for credit card payments or for monthly payments to pay all these unexpected expenses beyond what is available from the miscellaneous allocation.

- The IRS does not allow for continuing education, for private school tuition, or for college tuition.

- The IRS does not allow for tithing, charitable gifts, vacations, home improvements, or anything else that it deems will use up money that the IRS feels should be dedicated to paying delinquent taxes.

- Accounting and legal fees for representation before the IRS are allowable if they are reasonable and not excessive. Tax preparation expenses are also allowed. An example of reasonable is determined by the IRS on a case-by-case basis.

State and Local Taxes

Before contacting the IRS, state and local taxes should be dealt with first; because these agencies are usually much more aggressive than the IRS. The amounts due to the state and county are usually much less than what is due to the IRS. So, making a written agreement with the state or local tax authority will usually be honored by the IRS. The IRM addresses this in its usual lopsided interpretation of the law. This is critical information. *Taxpayers must make that agreement first, or IRS will not allow it later.* The IRS has to honor an "existing agreement for delinquent state or local tax debts," which was established before contacting the IRS.

Health Expenses

The out-of-pocket health care cannot be questioned. It changes every year. There is one amount if you are under 65 and another if you are over 65. Research shows that taxpayers spend more on medications, personal care objects, diabetes supplies, diapers, and other personal, health-related expenses. This may also include the cost of transportation to get to and from doctor and hospital visits.

The costs of medical marijuana are never allowed because marijuana is illegal according to federal law.

Child Care and Elderly Dependent Care Expenses

Some taxpayers have to pay for child care facilities to take care of their children or elderly relative while they are at work. Sometimes, they also use household help such as a nanny or babysitter to provide daily care for their children. The IRS may give a taxpayer a hard time about this and make judgments regarding the costs reported; however, the taxpayer has the right to choose who will watch their children when they cannot. With the receipts for care, even from occasional babysitters, the IRS should allow the expense in full.

NOTE: If a taxpayer states during any interview that they wish to consult with an authorized representative, the IRS employee will suspend the interview to permit such consultation.

EXHIBITS 11–14

Exhibit #11: *Collection National Standards*

2021 Allowable Living Expenses National Standards

Expense	One Person	Two Persons	Three Persons	Four Persons
Food	$400	$724	$838	$955
Housekeeping supplies	$41	$76	$69	$79
Apparel & services	$92	$150	$191	$249
Personal care products & services	$42	$76	$72	$89
Miscellaneous	$723	$1,292	$1,473	$1,740

More Than Four Persons	Additional Persons Amount
For each additional person, add four-person total allowance:	$341

Exhibit #12: *2021 Allowable Living Expenses Health Care Standards*

2021 Allowable Living Expanses Health Care Standards

	Out of Pocket Costs
Under 65	$68
65 and Older	$142

Exhibit #13: *Local Standards Housing and Utilities*

Local Standards Housing and Utilities

Disclaimer: IRS Collection Financial Standards are intended for use in calculating repayment of delinquent taxes. These Standards are effective on April 26, 2021 for purposes of federal tax administration only. Expense information for use in bankruptcy calculations can be found on the website for the US Trustee Program.

The housing and utilities standards are derived from US Census Bureau, American Community Survey and Bureau of Labor Statistics data, and are provided by state down to the county level. The standard for a particular county and family size includes both housing and utilities allowed for a taxpayer's primary place of residence. Generally, the total number of persons allowed for determining family size should be the same as those allowed as exemptions on the taxpayer's most recent year income tax return.

Housing and utilities standards include mortgage or rent, property taxes, interest, insurance, maintenance, repairs, gas, electric, water, heating oil, garbage collection, residential telephone service, cell phone service, cable television, and Internet service. The tables include five categories for one, two, three, four, and five or more persons in a household.

The taxpayer is allowed the standard amount, or the amount actually spent on housing and utilities, whichever is less. If the amount claimed is more than the total allowed by the housing and utilities standards, the taxpayer must provide documentation to substantiate those expenses are necessary living expenses.

Maxiumum Monthly Allowance

County	2021 Published Housing and Utilities for a Family of 1	2021 Published Housing and Utilities for a Family of 2	2021 Published Housing and Utilities for a Family of 3	2021 Published Housing and Utilities for a Family of 4	2021 Published Housing and Utilities for a Family of 5
Alameda County	2,731	3,208	3,380	3,769	3,830
Alpine County	1,847	2,169	2,286	2,549	2,590
Amador County	1,762	2,070	2,181	2,432	2,471
Butte County	1,650	1,938	2,042	2,277	2,314
Calaveras County	1,860	2,185	2,302	2,567	2,608
Colusa County	1,609	1,889	1,991	2,220	2,256
Contra Costa County	2,575	3,024	3,187	3,554	3,611
Del Norte County	1,450	1,703	1,794	2,000	2,033
El Dorado County	2,187	2,569	2,707	3,018	3,067
Fresno County	1,643	1,929	2,033	2,267	2,303
Glenn County	1,548	1,818	1,916	2,136	2,171
Humboldt County	1,736	2,038	2,148	2,395	2,434
Imperial County	1,498	1,759	1,854	2,067	2,101
Inyo County	1,845	2,168	2,284	2,547	2,588
Kern County	1,555	1,827	1,925	2,146	2,181
Kings County	1,499	1,760	1,855	2,068	2,102
Lake County	1,584	1,860	1,960	2,185	2,221
Lassen County	1,490	1,750	1,844	2,056	2,089
Los Angeles County	2,367	2,780	2,929	3,266	3,319

Madera County	1,576	1,851	1,950	2,174	2,209
Marin County	3,332	3,914	4,124	4,598	4,672
Mariposa County	1,666	1,957	2,062	2,299	2,336
Mendocino County	1,873	2,200	2,318	2,585	2,626
Merced County	1,527	1,794	1,890	2,107	2,141
Modoc County	1,239	1,455	1,533	1,709	1,737
Mono County	1,827	2,146	2,261	2,521	2,562
Monterey County	2,174	2,553	2,690	2,999	3,048
Napa County	2,509	2,947	3,105	3,462	3,518
Nevada County	2,045	2,402	2,531	2,822	2,868
Orange County	2,610	3,065	3,230	3,601	3,660
Placer County	2,267	2,663	2,806	3,129	3,179
Plumas County	1,556	1,828	1,926	2,147	2,182
Riverside County	1,950	2,290	2,413	2,690	2,734
Sacramento County	1,892	2,223	2,342	2,611	2,653
San Benito County	2,384	2,800	2,951	3,290	3,343
San Bernardino County	1,773	2,082	2,194	2,446	2,486
San Diego County	2,430	2,855	3,008	3,354	3,408
San Francisco County	3,331	3,912	4,122	4,596	4,670
San Joaquin County	1,874	2,201	2,319	2,586	2,627
San Luis Obispo County	2,245	2,637	2,779	3,099	3,149
San Mateo County	3,235	3,800	4,004	4,464	4,537

Santa Barbara County	2,257	2,651	2,793	3,114	3,164
Santa Clara County	3,108	3,651	3,847	4,289	4,359
Santa Cruz County	2,642	3,103	3,270	3,646	3,705
Shasta County	1,611	1,892	1,994	2,223	2,259
Sierra County	1,554	1,825	1,923	2,144	2,179
Siskiyou County	1,390	1,632	1,720	1,918	1,949
Solano County	2,093	2,458	2,590	2,888	2,934
Sonoma County	2,321	2,726	2,872	3,202	3,254
Stanislaus County	1,702	2,000	2,107	2,349	2,387
Sutter County	1,681	1,975	2,081	2,320	2,358
Tehama County	1,458	1,713	1,805	2,013	2,045
Trinity County	1,495	1,756	1,850	2,063	2,096
Tulare County	1,466	1,721	1,814	2,023	2,055
Tuolumne County	1,740	2,044	2,154	2,402	2,440
Ventura County	2,426	2,850	3,003	3,348	3,402
Yolo County	2,140	2,514	2,649	2,954	3,001
Yuba County	1,681	1,975	2,081	2,320	2,358

Exhibit #14: *Allowable Living Expenses Transportation Standards*

Allowable Living Expenses Transportation Standards

	Public Transportation	
National	$217	
	Ownership Costs	
	One Car	Two Cars
National	$533	$1,055
	Operating Costs	
	One Car	Two Cars
Northeast Region	$274	$548
Boston	$271	$542
New York	$355	$710
Philadelphia	$293	$586
Midwest Region	$201	$402
Chicago	$226	$452
Cleveland	$201	$402
Detroit	$305	$610
Mionneapolis-St. Paul	$203	$406
St. Louis	$233	$466
South Region	$224	$448
Atlanta	$251	$502
Baltimore	$262	$524
Dallas-Ft. Worth	$277	$554
Houston	$309	$618
Miami	$379	$758
Tampa	$238	$476
Washington, D.C.	$247	$494
West Region	$242	$484
Anchorage	$203	$406
Denver	$267	$534
Honolulu	$210	$420

Operating Costs, cont.		
	One Cars	Two Cars
Los Angeles	$313	$626
Pheonix	$246	$492
San Diego	$280	$560
San Francisco	$267	$534
Seattle	242	$484

CHAPTER 14

WHY IS YOUR CASE ASSIGNED TO A REVENUE OFFICER?

The good news for many right now is that after years of retirements and no new hiring and budget cuts, there are only 1,776 bag carrying *Revenue Officers* left in the field. There used to be 11,314 Collection Employees. So, if you owe taxes, your chance of ever seeing a *Revenue Officer* is reduced. But you are probably reading this chapter because a R/O has contacted you.

What is a *Revenue Officer*?

For 33 years, my job as an IRS *Senior Revenue Officer* required me to make cold calls to individuals and businesses that had not filed tax returns or paid income, employment taxes, or other taxes.

Revenue Officers (R/O) are the pride of the IRS. They are the chief enforcers in the field. These are the most highly trained employees in IRS Collection Division and are paid well. They work on all cases that the *Service Center Pipeline* or *Automation Collection System* cannot resolve. This elite force has advanced training and knowledge and works to collect unpaid taxes, and is powerful and effective in promoting tax compliance. *Revenue Officers* collect individual high-income tax balances (over $250,000) and business and employment taxes. *Revenue Officers* work the most complex collection cases and work one on one with taxpayers. When needed, they can levy assets and seize real property or other assets—like businesses

Cases are primarily sorted and assigned based upon their tax balances. Revenue Officer's inventories can become "clogged up" with cases of bankrupt individuals and defunct businesses that show large tax balances due to them. This is wasted energy because the money isn't there to collect.

Revenue Officers should be redirected to the cases of *Rich People, Big Businesses, and Corporations* that are currently not paying their share of payroll and income taxes that are more easily collected in a timely fashion.

In the past, *Revenue Officers* were a reliable "boots on the ground" IRS presence in every city and town across the United States. They gave the public an actual person they could speak to, even if they did not always agree on the case resolution. The visibility of the *Revenue Officers* helped promote tax filing and paying compliance by the American citizen. It is no secret that people who have interacted with a *Revenue Officer* on any level will have a story to tell. It's the "snowball effect." One IRS contact shared with friends, family, and neighbors' bolsters tax compliance over a large geographic area.

Conversely, those parties who do not voluntarily file and pay their taxes (when a business withholds employment taxes from their employees but intentionally fails to pay them to the IRS) also learn a lot about the IRS system through social channels. This feeds the steady growth of tax evasion and non-compliance. Think of it like sending a petty criminal to a criminals' college. These individuals learn the trick of evading their civic responsibilities.

How Do I Know I Have a *Revenue Officer*?

Before Covid-19, the first time you meet your *Revenue Officer* in person is when they come knocking on your front door unannounced. This could be at your home or business address. However, *Revenue Officers* have not made field calls since March 2020 and are not expected to resume making field calls until Fall 2021. To start, *Revenue Officers* will judge you—how you talk, act, and look. Then they will evaluate your lifestyle, the jewelry you are wearing, including watches, or anything else that might indicate a more elaborate lifestyle. Just so you know, "bling" especially catches their eye. The *Revenue Officers* want to see what you own. This is a good reason not to let them into your home to interview you. While standing in your doorway, the *Revenue Officers* make sure they note if you are cooperative and want to pay and willingly work with them.

Usually, only one *Revenue Officer* comes to your door, and they will switch between the "good cop–bad cop" routine. Sometimes they talk one way (friendly) to you and another way (harshly) at other times, depending on what they want you to do and how fast they want it done. If you are cooperative, you should have a good experience. Unfortunately, when their manager reviews your case or when your case is over a year old, they become very aggressive, and if you do not do everything they want, they start levying your income and assets. If you ignore *the Revenue Officer*—you will quickly feel the pain of their enforced collection actions. The *Revenue Officer* standing at your door may threaten to return and remove all your possessions.

Here is where you should hire a tax professional to speak for you. You have rights. You have the *Collection Appeals Program* and the right for a *Collection Due Process Appeal*. You can also open up a case with the *IRS National Taxpayer Advocate*.

Additionally, you can also contact your Congressperson, Senator, or the White House and ask them to advocate for you. That is free, and if you have a good argument for an *Installment Agreement* or *Currently Not Collectible*, they can help you. You have rights explained in bureaucratic detail in the *IRS Collection Process Publication 594* and *Publication 1 Your Rights as a Taxpayer* (Google search). These publications discuss the collection process, payment options, federal tax liens, appeal rights, and summons. A summons is used by the IRS when you do not cooperate or provide the information, they require to verify your financial condition. A summons legally compels you or some third party (like your bank or credit card company) to meet with the IRS and provide information, documents, and testimony. These are used to force you to provide the *Collection Information Statements, Form 433-A or Form 433-B*.

If you cannot attend, you must respond to the IRS in writing to request a new time to appear. If you do not appear, the IRS can go to Federal District Court and sue you to comply with the summons. At this point, some people have still refused to give financial information and have ended up in jail. I have worked cases on some of these belligerent taxpayers.

The IRS wants *Revenue Officers* only to work the most critical, complex, and technical cases. You and your case must be very important to be assigned an R/O. It's the opposite of winning the lottery.

The IRS tax collector will always look for your Achilles heel, your weak spot. If you lie to the *Revenue Officer* or fail to do what you commit to doing, you can expect what you are most afraid of—a levy on your bank or wages where your money is withdrawn by the IRS order. The bank will charge you for the seizure of your funds, adding insult to injury. Effective *Revenue Officers* are always thinking about their next action. They assume that whatever the taxpayer says will not happen, and the R/O will have to take enforced collection actions.

The IRS sends you many letters, but eventually-now that Covid-19 is passing, an IRS *Revenue Officer* will show up at your door without warning. It is never at a convenient time. They don't care. There is a reason for that. They want to see how you live and to see what you have so they can take it.

Picture this. It's Friday afternoon, and you're leaving for dinner with the in-laws. The *Revenue Officer* is at your door. The R/O will attempt to talk to you and may seem friendly but in a pushy, nosy way. They will ask the most personal questions about your lifestyle, relationships, living arrangements, questions about your style of living, marital status, and children. They will want to see inside your house and business to look for other assets, like artwork or antique furniture that can be seized. Meanwhile, you are worried about being late for your in-laws and try to rush the process. This is a critical error on your part.

You need to know what a R/O can do to you, so pay attention. Stop and think. Call and cancel any activities. Call your tax accountant. A Revenue Officer can destroy what's left of your life if you are not doing what they want fast enough. They do this by filing a *Notice of Federal Tax Lien* against you and taking your wages, income, bank account, cars, trucks, and equity in your house. Plus, they can take anything else that you own—all without going to Court. They have power over you, so respect that upfront.

Revenue Officers can be professional, reasonable, and compassionate as long as they think that you are cooperating with them. However, if you are not cooperating or are disrespectful in any way, they can make your life miserable, filling your life with worry, fear, and anxiety. There are many avenues of appeals that you can use to get a second opinion on the actions taken by the R/O. However, remember, most of their supervisors you are appealing to were formerly R/O's.

The IRS *Revenue Officer* is a person you should always believe—if they warn you that they will do something—they will. Never lie, attempt to deceive, or mess with *Revenue Officers* in any way.

Suppose a case cannot be resolved in the *Service Center Collection Pipeline* or *Automated Collection System*. In that case, it goes into the *Revenue Officer Field Queue*—a holding place waiting for a *Revenue Officer* to become available to work the case. It sits there for 52 weeks. Then the manager must decide if it should be issued to an actual *Revenue Officer* or if the case will be Shelved. Being Shelved means it goes into an inactive file and will probably never be worked again. You still owe the taxes and will continue to receive a yearly balance due letter (*CP71A*), and any future yearly tax refunds will be applied to old taxes due.

This potential shelving is again possible because of the lack of current *Revenue Officers*. In my present tax business client inventory, I have 11 clients who owe more than $1 million and have not been contacted beyond the stream of yearly IRS letters for years. Yet, I have dozens of clients who owe less than $100,000 who are contacted all the time by the IRS. This means they are put into an active collection system with several yearly letters from the IRS and constant telephone calls.

The Treasury Inspector General reported that at that time, the IRS had 2,038 experienced *Revenue Officers* actively working 108,000 cases. 85% of those cases were classified as a high priority. However, the *Revenue Officer Queue* had another 649,000 that were high priority cases that were awaiting assignment to the dwindling number of *Revenue Officers*. If I were to estimate, there are only 1,776 *Revenue Officers* left at this time. Most of the cases in *Queue* are for amounts in the millions of dollars, and it is likely that they will never be worked because there are not enough IRS bodies to handle the cases.

Cases That a *Revenue Officer* Must Work Per the Internal Revenue Manual (IRM)

Cases that cannot be moved to the *Queue* and must be worked by a *Revenue Officer* are listed below:

- Businesses and individuals that have defaulted on an *Installment Agreement* (IA's)—this is very important. Defaulted IAs are always a top priority. Think very carefully before you make an *Installment Agreement* with the IRS because you will always be at the top of the IRS list after that. (Please review Chapter 10)
- A business that has not paid its *Employment Taxes (Form 940, 941, or 944 taxes)*. The case gets a higher priority if the business owes for two or more quarters. IRS calls these cases "tax repeaters" who are "pyramiding tax liabilities." That is, when a business withholds employment taxes from their employees but intentionally fails to pay them to the IRS.
- Cases on government employees or retirees who have tax delinquencies
- Cases on high-income taxpayers (incomes over $100,000)
- Cases with a balance due of $250,000 or above
- *Trust Fund Recovery Penalty (TFRP)* over $250,000
- Cases of prominent individuals, politicians
- Nationally known high-profile individuals
- Entertainers
- Sports figures

- Promoters
- Other influential individuals or businesses
- Return preparer penalty cases
- Global High Wealth (GHW) individuals with over $10 million in annual income
- Accountants, Lawyers, Judges, and financial institutions.

If you have been doing something that the IRS believes was a way to take money from the US Treasury illegally or your case hints at tax evasion, my advice would be to consult a tax professional.

How to Negotiate with Your *Revenue Officer*

Remember, in the eyes of the IRS, you are always "guilty until you prove yourself innocent."

Clichés really are true! "Talk is cheap" with *Revenue Officers*: "Actions speak louder than words," and "Numbers never lie." All apply here. The Revenue Officer will want a full *Form 433-A Collection Financial Statement* from you and *Form 433-B* from your business. They will evaluate your income and expenses and your lifestyle. They will allow you certain amounts for food, clothing, housing, and transportation, as mentioned previously in Chapter 10. Remember, expenses can be negotiable depending on the circumstances of your life.

In your negotiation process, I suggest that you first clean up your finances. The IRS does not care if you live comfortably or have savings or retirement security—it wants its money. The IRS views it as when you failed to pay your taxes; you sold off a part of yourself to the United States Government.

The most dangerous power that the *Revenue Officer* has over you is their ability to take what you have through a seizure and public sale: house equity, car(s), stocks, bonds, business interests, etc. They can and have taken it all before. They have done this since 1865.

However, the IRS staff is so decimated in their ranks that they did only 228 seizures in 2019, down 17% from the year before.

IRS did 10,000 seizures in the year 2000. But the IRS, including the *Revenue Officers*, filed 543,604 liens. These liens can destroy a person's credit scores and ability to get jobs and buy and sell their homes. This can destroy your life for years to come.

In 2020 there were only 77 seizures (down 66%). And only 291,081 liens were filed (down 53%). The number of levies issued was 782,735 and now has dropped down to only 396,269. Down 51% So this truly is the **"The Best Time Ever to Owe the IRS!"**

The Treasury Inspector General showed that in 56 of the seizures, the taxpayers were "low-income indicators." That means people who owned some asset, usually a house, could not get a mortgage because their income was too low. The seizures happened, even though the taxpayer claimed that they were experiencing "economic hardship." Twenty-one of the seizures were personal residences. The rest were other real property, vehicles, and other business or personal property. If this, were you, you would be out on the street without transportation or financial security?

Before a seizure, *Revenue Officers* must first explore "*alternate methods of resolution.*" These are voluntary payment, *Installment Agreement*, voluntarily selling or borrowing against an asset or an IA. (See Chapter 10).

As a senior R/O, I was involved in 100 seizures and the personal tragedies that resulted in six suicides that will haunt me forever.

CHAPTER 15

WHAT KIND OF DEALS CAN YOU MAKE WITH IRS COLLECTION?

There are many *Installment Agreement* options offered by the IRS:

- You can get an *online Installment Agreement* if you can pay within the next 120 days. There is no service charge, no financial statement required, and no *Notice of Federal Tax Lien*.

- The *Automatic Guaranteed Installment Agreement* is used for cases with balances of $10,000 or less (*excluding* penalties and interest) that can be paid within 36 months. There is no financial statement required as well as no *Notice of Federal Tax Lien* required. You can apply online. A service charge applies of approximately $250.

- One *Streamlined Installment Agreement* is for cases that owe $10,001 to $25,000 tax (*including* penalties and interest). The payments can be spread out over 72 months. This agreement is offered even if the taxpayer can fully pay today per IRM 5.14.5.2. No financial statement and no *Notice of Federal Tax Lien* is filed. The *Streamlined Installment Agreement* is for personal income taxes and business income taxes under $25,000. A service charge applies of approximately $250.

Chapter 15: What Kind of Deals Can You Make with the IRS Collection?

- Another *Streamlined Installment Agreement* is for cases between $25,001 to $50,000 tax owed. The IRS will allow you 72 months to pay. The IRS will require you to submit either *Collection Financial Statement Form 433-A* or *Form 433-F*, and they will decide about filing a lien against you. The IRS wants more financial information, and you will need to provide a *Collection Information Statement* (CIS) and get the *Notice of Federal Tax Lien*, which are more intrusive in your life. Individuals and defunct businesses can both qualify for this agreement. This agreement is much discussed in media commercials that offer tax help and is called the *IRS Fresh Start Program*. This was introduced in 2012 and raised the dollar amounts for *Installment Agreements* and *Offers in Compromise*. As usual, the IRS made the *Fresh Start Program* complicated. The *Fresh Start Program* does not offer much benefit to most taxpayers. It is not much of a "Fresh Start" because it does not reduce the tax balance or remove any penalties or interest.

All other *Installment Agreements* apply to balances over $25,000 that "cannot" be fully paid in 72 months or "cannot" be fully paid before the *Collection Statue of Expiration* expires. *Form 433-F* is required for *Automated Collection System* cases (ACS). *Form 433-A* or *Form 433-B* is required for cases being worked on by the *Field Collection*. A *Federal Tax Lien* is optional up to $50,000 but required over $50,000.

For any of these categories, the taxpayer can make a lump sum payment to reduce their account to the amount within the IRS guidelines for types of agreements. For example, if you owe $30,000 and pay $5,000, the *Installment Agreement* terms will be more favorable to you, not the IRS. This is a significant change because, in the past, the IRS did not let you do this.

If you have an *Installment Agreement* on any amount over $10,001, which will not be fully paid before the *Collection Statute of Expirations* time (ten years from the date the tax was assessed), this is called a Part Pay Installment Agreement (PPIA). A *Notice of Federal Tax Lien* is required to be filed.

Types of Business Taxes and How to Work with the IRS

- *In-Business Trust Fund Taxes* are taxes that a currently operating business owes, and these are for *Form 941* (employment taxes) only. An *Express Installment Agreement* ($10,000 or below) is covered under *Automatic Guaranteed Installment Agreement* just mentioned and offers 24 months to pay fully. A *Notice of Federal Tax Lien* may be filed, but it is unlikely if the balance is under $25,000.

- *In-Business Trust Fund Taxes* for amounts over $10,001 to $25,000 must be paid within 24 months thru a *Direct Debit Installment Agreement*. No financial statement is required. However, a *Notice of Federal Tax Lien* is usually required to be filed.

For example, suppose you owe corporate income taxes or owe employment taxes on a corporation that is now out of business. In that case, you are not legally required to pay those taxes because they are a corporate entity's debt and not your personal debt. You are likely to be assessed the *Trust Fund Recovery Penalty* if you owe employment taxes. Once those are assessed against you, they become your personal taxes.

Our businessman, Jim, owes $100,000 in business employment taxes for his plumbing company. He received an IRS letter telling him he owes $75,000 in employment taxes for his company. However, his plumbing company still owes $100,000. Poor Jim now owes an additional $75,000. Although the IRS will try to collect *both* the $100,000 from the company and $75,000 from Jim, yet the IRS will stop the collection process at $100,000. Is this confusing? You bet! Jim needs to consult a tax professional immediately to understand his rights and responsibilities.

If you continue to "pyramid" (not pay your taxes quarter after quarter) while screaming "no more new taxes," or you do not file future tax returns and make Federal Tax Deposits, then you will face continuing IRS enforced collection actions. If you are still in business, the IRS can seize the funds from your bank account every 30 days, can levy your credit card processing company every day, and also seize your daily receipts.

Service Charge for Installment Agreements

All *installment agreements* come with a service charge of $120 (for a regular installment agreement or with a *Payroll Deduction Installment Agreement*). If you are paying with a *Direct Debit Installment Agreement*, the service charge is $52. Low-income taxpayers can get a reduced rate of $43. Use Google to search for *Form 13844, Application for Reduced User Fee for Installment Agreements*.

You need to know that even if you have an *installment agreement*, you are still charged with a *Failure to File Penalty* and a *Failure to Pay Penalty*. The *Failure to Pay Penalty* will continue to accrue until the tax is paid in full. It may be to your advantage to wait until you fully pay the tax due before requesting penalty relief under the IRS *first-time penalty abatement policy*.

Each penalty rates are up to 25% of the balance, plus 3% interest (which is compounded daily and continues to be charged for the length of the agreement). In a worst-case scenario, if the balance owed is $100,000, then $25,000 or 25% plus for failure to file penalty, another $25,000 for failure to pay penalty plus $300 (3%) interest. You do the math. Your ship has sunk. The good news is that any payments that you make are applied to the tax first.

The *Service Center Collection* works cases up to $25,000 for business taxes and up to $50,000 for personal income taxes. Generally, if the *Service Center Collection* is unable to resolve the case due to the amounts being above $50,000, it will transfer your case to the *Automated Collection System* (ACS).

The ACS works cases up to $100,000. The ACS sends high or medium-risk cases to the *Queue* after 26 weeks. For example, the IRS prioritizes the cases by the income reported, the balance due or expected balance due in non-filers, and includes other factors such as if the case is for an individual or a business.

Low-risk cases are not sent to the *Queue* but are *Shelved by National Office* after 104 weeks. If ACS cannot contact you or work with you, depending on the type of case, they will transfer your case directly to a *Field Revenue Officer* or to the *Queue* for *Field Collection*. This is based on the priorities that the IRS establishes. One priority is a business that is in operation, has employees, and is not paying in the money that was withheld from the employees.

The *Queue* system is relatively new and it has major flaws in the sense that the low-risk cases are assigned by the computer coding. This means that after 104 weeks, they are automatically removed from the *Shelved/ Queue* and sent to a private collection agency. The IRS has turned over their responsibilities to private companies, which cost the taxpayers more money than if the IRS kept their cases in house. This appears to be contrived to feed those members of Congress who want to help out their friends who run collection agencies.

All cases over $100,000 are transferred to the *Queue* where they wait to be issued to a *Field Revenue Officer*. Some are transferred directly to a *Field Revenue Officer* because they are deemed high risk, such as well-known persons.

Three Types of Installment Agreements

- The *Standard Installment Agreement* is where you send a check or make a payment using *Electronic Federal Tax Payment System* (EFTPS) every month.

- The *Payroll Deduction Installment Agreement* is one you should **never agree** to. It is extra work for your employer and presents many problems. It could lead to you losing your job. Besides, it makes no sense to let your employer in on your private business, and the IRS cannot force this type of agreement on you.

- The *Direct Debit Installment Agreement (DDIA)* is where the IRS takes the money out of your checking account every month. This type of agreement is almost impossible to stop. I suggest that you open a checking account at a different bank and use it solely to make the *installment agreement* payments. This advice is given because things happen in your personal and financial lives every day, and you need to be in the best position to handle that. For example, if you are now unemployed and barely able to pay bills, a normal IRS *DDIA* would just keep drawing the money out of your account. After you are in an *installment agreement,* you can expect little or no customer service because the employee you are talking to has no control over your case. The IRS is not flexible or accommodating. A *DDIA* can take up to 6 months before the IRS inputs the debits. So, taxpayers should mail a monthly check in the meantime.

When you near the 10-year mark where you will no longer owe on this tax, you will want to send a certified letter to the IRS stating this and request the IRS to stop withdrawing funds.

If you choose a *DDIA*, it can currently take the IRS six to eight months to input it on their system, so you may need to make manual payments in the meantime. Again, this means you may need to write monthly checks until you are in the system.

If the IRS has already filed a lien against you, and if you are in a *DDIA*, they will consider withdrawing the Notice of Federal Tax Lien if you have made two months' payments. Search for *Form 12277—Application for Withdrawal of Filed Form 668 (Y), Notice of Federal Tax Lien.* The problem is that the lien has already shown up on your credit report. A Federal Tax Lien will cause any credit that you can still get to come with high interest rates since you are a credit risk. The *Notice Form 12277* is just stating that the IRS is pulling back its lien, not that you don't still owe the money. However, the IRS may also withdraw the lien if it helps you pay your taxes more quickly. Potential lenders think of it this way: "This person did not pay the IRS; why would they pay me back either?"

Liens cause people to lose their existing jobs, lose their ability to be licensed, bonded, and insured, lose their security clearance and cause future employers to shy away from hiring them.

Even if you have a lien against your home, it can be "discharged" or "subordinated." That means that the IRS will take the equity in your home and then allow you to sell it. Or, if you are trying to refinance your mortgage, the IRS may allow a new mortgage to jump ahead and take priority over the Federal Tax Lien. This is because it will allow the taxpayer to pay more money to the IRS.

In all types of installment agreements, you need to know that any future tax refunds you have will automatically be held by the IRS and applied to your back taxes. If this causes you a hardship, you can file a new *W-9 Form* claiming more exemptions. This will reduce your refund and give you more income throughout the year, which can be used to pay your agreement.

Form 9465 Applying for an Installment Agreement

To apply for an *Installment Agreement*, use Google to search for *Form 9465*.

You can print and mail it in, or you can apply online. This is for a streamlined installment agreement that provides up to 72 months to pay your taxes including penalties, and interest. The IRS will let you know within 60 days if they approve of your agreement proposal or not.

If you have had an *Installment Agreement* in the past and defaulted on it, or if you owe more than $25,000 but less than $50,000, you must agree to either a *Direct Debt Installment Agreement (DDIA)* or a *Payroll Deduction Agreement*.

If you owe more than $50,000, you must complete *Form 433-F*. This is a *Collection Information Statement* that is not as detailed as *Form 433-A, Form 433-A Officer in Compromise* (OIC), and the *Form 433-B*. This form is only used by *Service Center Collection* and *Automated Collection System* (ACS). Revenue Officers will not accept it. Conversely, the Service Center and ACS will not accept the more complete *Form 433-A OIC* either.

Throughout this book, I advise you to complete *Form 433-A Offer in Compromise* and make sure that you get credit for all of your expenses because the *Form 433-F* does not give you that knowledge or opportunity. So, do *Form 433-A Offer in Compromise* first and then take what you need out of it to complete the *Form 433-F*. It will save you big money.

If you do not agree to pay by direct debit or payroll deduction, you must complete *Form 433-F* and file it with this form.

If the balance of taxes for all years is not more than $50,000, you do not need to file *Form 9465*; you can just complete the *installment agreement* online.

If it seems like the IRS complicates the *installment agreement* process, remember that nothing is ever simple in the IRS.

When choosing a date for your *installment agreement*, I always suggest you start it two months after the application date because it really takes the IRS time to look at your request and approve it. They can always say no, but at least you will have asked for those terms. For example, if today is June 10, then make your payment date proposal August 15. You can only choose a payment date from the 1st to the 28th of the month.

Never double up on your payments. Don't do this because the IRS computer does not understand. The computer expects payment from you every month by a specific date. If you make two to three payments all at once, it does not care; you still need to make the payment on time next month. If you do make additional payments, it will help you, but don't count on the idea of pre-paying your *installment agreement*.

If you cannot make your payment, you need to know a secret that the IRS does not tell you. The *installment agreement* system has a one-time automatic skip payment built into it. It will not default your agreement. This is very important if you are under financial stress. You do not need to call, but you can send a letter saying you missed the payment and why and plan to resume the payments the next month. Send this certified letter to the IRS and keep a copy yourself.

If the IRS is Not Calling You, Then Why Are You Calling Them?

No one will have direct access to your case. If you call, no record will be made of your call. No one can help you because you are in the "Master Computer." The IRS computer is impossible to communicate with; it only understands actions. If you do not pay, it understands that you are starting to default your agreement and will send you a terse warning letter.

What You Expect from the Service Center

If you call *Service Center Collection*, the IRS agent will first verify who you are, where you work, and where you bank. The agent has a very structured interview and will ask if you have your monthly income and expense information. For most people, this is a shock because they are not thinking they needed their financial papers in front of them. You were just calling to see what could be done about the back taxes. You did not expect to be launched into making an *installment agreement*. You usually don't know and don't remember all the expenses you pay out every month.

As a result, you end up agreeing to an *installment agreement* for a much higher amount than you can afford.

Service Center Collection cannot issue levies to seize anything, but they do make notes on their system regarding what you called about, what you said, and how you acted. That record will determine how you will be treated in the future. If you are rude or disrespectful, it will come back to bite you later. Make sure to use appropriate language and be respectful by remembering the IRS agent is just doing their job.

All of these things are why you need to complete *Form 433-A Officer in Compromise* **before you call.**

That will allow you the time to research what the IRS really allows you for all of your monthly expenses. **This is the secret to gaining the maximum advantage in your IRS negotiations**, because some months you will have expenses that change, i.e., car repairs., medical expenses, life's emergencies, etc.

If the IRS employee you are speaking to is rude, intimidating, or makes you uncomfortable or stressed-out and the interview is not going in your favor, just hang up. No need to explain or give notice. For the IRS, it is another lost call; it's no big deal. Then, you can get yourself together and call back. Again, these calls are not recorded. The "collection roulette" will offer you another employee. If you are better prepared, then maybe you will get lucky the second time and

Chapter 15: What Kind of Deals Can You Make with the IRS Collection?

negotiate a better payment plan. But first, let me be clear, you need to remember what I already addressed earlier in the book, **be calm, patient, and respectful.**

You must be ready to tell your story and make the IRS come around your way of thinking. Once again, I cannot stress strongly enough; you must not be rude, belligerent, use swear words, or ask for something that the IRS simply cannot give you. That is why you are reading this book; you need to find out what your options are.

Service Center Collection is not known for having a "big heart." In fact, their Internal Revenue Manual advises its employees, "If the taxpayer states that they are having financial difficulty, ask them if they can make a minimum payment of $25 a month and increase it over time". Wait! What? You just established you don't have money and still they want money?

Now you are beginning to see what you are up against. The best IRS employees do what they are told to do, and in *Service Center Collection* and *Automatic Collection System* (ACS), there are boilerplate scripts for them to use in questioning taxpayers. These do not allow for the human factor to play many parts in their case decisions.

What You Can Expect from Automatic Collection System (ACS)

This next part can get confusing. If you owe over $50,000 in income taxes, then the Service Center Collection may not be able to help you. They will transfer the case to the *Queue* (the holding place) leading into *ACS*.

It might take some time for you to be contacted. In all the phases of collection, high tax dollar balances always go to the head of the line. You can still send in payments even without an agreement. Just put your Social Security Number on the face of the check and the tax year where you want it applied. The IRS must post the check where you want it to go.

The *ACS* generally will work cases from $25,000 to $100,000. That is for income taxes. *Employment taxes (Form 941)* have lower dollar thresholds because they are due every quarter. This means that they can rapidly pyramid (increase) into large balances, and thus they receive more immediate attention. Employment tax cases over $25,000 usually will be assigned to a *Field Revenue Officer.*

Form 433-F—Collection Information Statement is the only form that *Automated Collection System* and the *Service Center Collection* use. It seems silly, but that is how they were trained. The problem with the *Collection Information Statement* is that it does not explain your rights to claim full credit for the *National Allowable Expenses* approved for your area. I have advised many people how to utilize *Form 433-F Collection Information Statement* in my practice. Because the IRS will allow your car payments and rent expenses to be higher than you may have, it makes sense to buy a new car or upgrade your living arrangements. For example, if you owe taxes and you are living in your parent's spare bedroom not paying rent, the IRS will not allow you rent credit. If you have a lease with your parents, which includes utilities, then the IRS will allow it. Another way to maximize your advantage in lifestyle is to rent an apartment and have the IRS allow you that expense plus utilities, especially in cases where it is unlikely that you will ever be able to pay the taxes in full. At the very least, you will retain a living place.

Everything you just read for *Service Center Collection* applies double because the person in the *Automated Collection System* (ACS) has their finger on the LEVY BUTTON. The "levy button" is an actual process that automatically takes your bank account or wages. If you get the agent irritated, they will end the interview and send all the appropriate letters so that they can take your bank account, wages, salary, and any other income that you have.

The cases in *Automated Collection System* are never assigned to an individual employee. Employees just work whatever calls come in. However, the IRS agent may ask you to send some verification to their secret "eFax" telephone number if you are well prepared with your financial data. If you can get this secret number, then you can work with the same agent on that day only. There is no master list, even within the IRS, of these phone numbers. If you can get the information to them either by mail or using the eFax, the same person will review it and then make a decision on your tax matter.

Chapter 15: What Kind of Deals Can You Make with the IRS Collection?

Otherwise, a different agent will take the case from the first agent. The IRS does not use email for collection cases. Thus, this is the only way you can get a message directly to the person with whom you spoke to that day. This information might include copies of bills that seem high to the IRS or copies of your last three month's bank statements. Then, they will tell you if your installment agreement is approved and the terms of the agreement.

The *Automated Collection System* transfers 23% of its cases, valued at $14.5 billion, to the *Queue* for the *Field Revenue Officer*. It closes 16% of its cases as *Shelved* by National Office, mostly for people who owe $5,000 or less. Those lucky taxpayers will lose future refunds but will not be worked in the active collection.

Again, taxpayers who owe over $1000 might find themselves involved with a private collection company who takes the time to harass you. Sometimes this harassment is daily and can affect your health and family.

My final thoughts are to be polite, have your financial papers ready, discuss your situation with a tax professional first before you call the IRS, and be prepared to do your civic duty.

CHAPTER 16
IRS TARGETS FOR THE YEARS 2021–2022

The IRS has created a number of targets to focus on for 2021-2022. These targets are serious as the United States requires money to run the government. The IRS announced who they plan to target in 2021-2022. Due to Congress cutting the IRS budget over the past 30 plus years, the IRS is currently all bark and no bite because of a lack of resources and employees. It appears that budget-cutting at the IRS is changing now due to the massive debt accumulation since President Trump passed the Tax Cuts and Jobs Act in 2017 that benefited *Rich People, Big Businesses, and Corporations* exponentially.

Small Business Taxpayers

The first target is small business taxpayers. The IRS knows that self-employed people rarely report all of their income; many overstate their expenses. 56% either underreport income or do not report any income at all. This is a big problem for the IRS. Unreported tax on small business income for individuals is estimated to be a $110 billion loss per year.

Crypto-Currency Holders

The second target is the crypto-currency holders. Many people are making money from this system of buying and selling currency.

They make income but do not pay any income taxes. Why? There is almost no audit or paper trail on crypto-currency, and most people fail to report any income from their trades. The IRS identifies this as noncompliance. Similar to small business owners, the IRS knows where there is no virtual currency information reporting (i.e., *W-2s, 1099s*) and where there is the potential for large gains, there is a high likelihood of noncompliance. How does the crypto-currency avoid noncompliance? You keep good paper records of your trades that account for your gains and losses.

The IRS just issued procedure on how to trace virtual currency transactions and how to seize cryptocurrency. See IRM 5.11.6.21.1 (05-26-2021). The IRS just seized $1.2 billion in crypto-currency in 2020.

Employers Who Don't Pay Payroll Taxes

The third target for 2021-2022 regards employers who don't payroll taxes. Almost 74% of the taxes collected in the US tax system come from withheld payroll taxes. When employers don't pay their payroll taxes, the US Treasury takes a double hit. First, the IRS does not get the employee's withheld income and Social Security taxes. Secondly, their employees will still receive their *W-2 Forms* and the IRS tax refunds due to them, even if the employer did not pay the IRS the taxes. The IRS views employer collection and nonpayment of employee's withholdings (called "trust fund" taxes) as stealing.

The loss of over half the Revenue Officers who investigate unpaid payroll taxes has allowed this non-collection of taxes to get out of control. These taxes grow into large balances because payrolls can occur every week or two. For example, a business that owes $25,000 in one quarter rapidly will owe $100,000 over four quarters. Most new businesses have poor capitalization (start-up money) and poor cash flow. As a result, they "borrow" from Uncle Sam to fund their daily operations. This belief in illegal borrowing (or stealing) hurts their business in the long run. It also makes for unfair competition in the marketplace for the other businesses who file and pay their taxes on time. Any business owner that fails to pay will have most of the taxes assessed against them personally under a process known as the *Trust Fund Recovery Penalty*. The worst violators face criminal prosecution.

People Who Stop Filing Tax Returns

The fourth target is against those people who stop filing tax returns. The IRS claims that non-filers only represent $39 billion in lost revenue annually to the US Treasury. Many tax experts disagree with this estimate and, in their opinion, believe it is too low. The big problem with non-filers is that they think they are free and clear of any IRS contact. They voluntarily leave the tax system for good. However, their name remains in the IRS computer system. Also, the IRS tolerance of non-filers erodes the integrity of the voluntary compliance system.

Taxpayers Who Owe More than $250,000

The fifth target is taxpayers who owe more than $250,000. Many high-tax debt taxpayers were put on hold because the IRS did not have the resources to chase them down. From 2010 to 2018, the IRS lost almost half of its field collection personnel (*Revenue Officers*). As a result, these taxpayers may believe that they, too, are free and clear.

High-income Taxpayers Will be Audited More

The sixth target is high-income taxpayers. The IRS plans to audit more people with income over $1 million. In the past, high-income taxpayers have experienced audit rates as high as 12% (2011). In 2018, the audit rate of high wealth taxpayers was 3.4%. The taxpayer can expect more high-income audits due to the IRS's political pressure and a good return on this investment of time and energy. The average amount owed on a high-income audit yield in 2018 was $115,259. For 2021, it is estimated by the Treasury Inspector General for Tax Administration that those high-income taxpayers have approximately $45.7 billion in unpaid taxes.

Earned Income Tax Credits

The seventh target is *Earned Income Tax Credits*. The *Earned Income Tax Credits* encourage people to work by the worker receiving payment on being employed. 25% of all *Earned Income Tax Credit* claims are fraudulent per the IRS. For example, people make up dependents to receive a larger payment. This is fraud, and this costs the government $17 billion a year, so they continue to audit this type of tax credit.

The IRS Will Not Target:

Employers Who Wrongly Classify Employees: Employers who treat employees as independent contractors. Employment tax audits are done by *Revenue Agents* and require a great deal of time. Only 0.14% of employment tax returns are audited.

S Corporations and Partnerships: The audit rate for S corps and partnerships is 0.2%. These types of audits are very complex and require IRS employees with a minimum of ten years' experience to compete with the high-powered tax professionals who represent them. Without the additional hiring of IRS *Revenue Agents* (R/A), this will continue to be a low audit area. But hiring new auditors is not enough because they need years of training and experience before they can cope with, understand and attack a problem audit case. Monte Jackal, a former IRS Attorney, said, "If the IRS started staffing up now, it would take them at least a decade to catch up. They don't have enough IRS agents with enough knowledge to know what they are looking at. They are so grossly overmatched, it's not funny." (NYT 6-13-2021)

People earning less than $25,000 are at least three times more likely to be audited than rich partnerships. Of the four million partnership returns filed in 2018, the IRS audited only 140 of them. It did not pursue 300 high-income taxpayers (some who were members of said partnerships) who together cost the agency $10 billion in unpaid taxes over a three-year period when they failed to file tax returns. This arrogance has to be stopped.

One estimate, as reported by the New York Times on June 13, 2021, shows that the United States loses $75 billion a year from investors failing to report their income correctly, at least some of which would probably be recovered if the IRS conducted more audits.

As targets go, the IRS depends upon the US Congress to fund the agency to train new agents and retain their current workforce. Despite fewer agents today, this does not imply that this trend will continue.

CHAPTER 17

HOW DO THE *RICH PEOPLE* GET AWAY WITH NOT PAYING TAXES?

Rich People use several ways to avoid paying taxes. The tax laws provide many legal loopholes. These come under many names, such as capital gains, inheritance tax, business taxes, etc.

If you earn wages, you pay all sorts of taxes that *Rich People* do not have to pay. For instance, they may earn big bucks, but they only pay Social Security taxes on the first $142,800 of their wages. However, you probably pay it on all of your wages because you earn less than $142,800 as a middle or lower-wage-earning citizen. By the way, if the *Rich People* paid Social Security tax on all of their income, Social Security would be securely funded.

Most *Rich People* own stock, and they only pay a tax when they sell the stock. This is called capital gains tax, and the rates are 0%, 15%, and 20%, depending upon various factors. If your income is $500,000, your tax rate is 37%. If you make $500,000 selling stock, the highest rate you are taxed is 20%.

For example, Jim is a multi-millionaire who owns a large portfolio of stocks. He has not paid any income taxes on the stocks, yet they rise in value each year. He wants to buy a house for $3 million and pay cash for it. But he has little cash, just the stock portfolio. He sells some stock that he has owned for years, so he will owe 20% *Long Term Capital Gains Tax*. He spent $1 million to buy the stock, he paid tax on that money initially. So, he will deduct $1 million out of the $1 million, that was his cost. So now he only needs to pay tax on $2 million. If Jim had earned $2 million from working, he would be paying 37% tax rate. But Capitol Gains Tax tops out at 20%. So, Congress saved Jim 17% over a person working for his money.

Rich People pay taxes on their business income, but in 2017, Congress said, "Wait! You already pay so much in income taxes; let's just not count 20% of your income as income at all." This is called the *qualified business income deduction*. Did you know that corporations are taxed at 21%? Also, for example, if you are a CPA, lawyer, financial planner, or stockbroker, you are taxed at 21%, while the average W-2 earner has a 37% tax on wages that are taken directly from their pay before they receive their check. The list of benefits that go to *Rich People* goes on and on.

All of these tax breaks have fancy-sounding names, and trying to explain how they work is complicated.

Why are *Rich People* treated differently? Because *Rich People* have petitioned, lobbied, and convinced Congress that they need certain tax breaks because it is already such a burden to be *Rich* that they need tax relief. They are very bold in their requests to Congress. This could be labeled as greed.

Members of Congress who do favors for their "country club" buddies, their gold partners, their fellow *Rich People* by tailoring the tax laws give *Rich People* so many tax loopholes that they effectively pay tax rates far lower on their income than working people. The result of Congress pandering to the wealthy has put the US into debt that increases each year.

Here is a factoid: the last time the US budget was balanced was under President Bill Clinton. He reduced the national debt from 49.5GDP down to 34.5 GDP by the end of his term. The gross national debt was $5.6 trillion in the year 2020. Our gross national debt as of this publication is $28.4 trillion.

Rich People, Big Businesses, and Corporations organize their finances around the tax laws. They seek to avoid taxes, and that is legal. "Avoid taxes" is the mantra of ethical tax planners. However, some people seek to evade taxes, and that is illegal.

The top 1% of *Rich People* account for at least 28% to as much as 70% of the tax gap, according to a report in the ***New York Times***.

Chapter 17: How Do the *Rich People* Get Away Without Paying Taxes?

In 2020 approximately $600 billion in taxes were paid by 90% of the people. Approximately $600 billion of taxes owed was not paid by 10% of the people. The "tax gap" is the $600 billion in unpaid taxes due. (See Chapter 17.)

As it has been said, there are hundreds of legal ways in the law to help *Rich People, Big Businesses, and Corporations* avoid paying their full share of taxes. I like to believe this situation should be based on a French phrase, "nobles oblige." This means that the noble (rich) people have a greater obligation to take care of the less fortunate than other people. Or, in other words, "To those who are given so much—much will be expected." (Luke 12:48). Sadly, somewhere along the way, this idea of "nobles oblige" was lost. Some might say it started to "go out the window" with Gordon Geeko proclaiming "Greed is Good!" in the 1987 movie "Wall Street."

Clearly, the *Rich People, Big Businesses, and Corporations* have a greater obligation to fund government programs that benefit all people. Likewise, *Rich People, Big Businesses, and Corporations* stand to continue to reap the most benefits from a strong democratic, capitalist economy. Unfortunately, the world has adopted a Kardashian modality that includes greed, vanity, lust, and a desire to display their great rewards instead of doing their civic duty and paying the appropriate amount of taxes.

But I am not a social reformer; I am just a taxpayer who wants to know that the IRS is being fair in monitoring all taxpayers and is aware of the foibles of human nature, which include the delusion that stealing money from "We the People" is good and just. I want everyone with an income to pay their "fair share" of the tax burden. Sadly, people have been fed this idea that the government is rotten and should not be supported through some media and in their mega-churches as well. Mega-rich pastors who purchase their airplanes, mansions, and Lamborghinis present an abomination to the message of Jesus Christ. "Then shall the King say unto them on his right hand, Come, ye blessed of my Father, inherit the kingdom prepared for you from the foundation of the world: For I was hungry, and ye gave me meat: I was thirsty, and ye gave me drink: I was a stranger, and ye took me in: Naked, and ye clothed me: I was sick, and ye visited me: I was in prison, and ye came unto me." (Matthew 25:34-36)

What is the Tax Gap?

Simple. The tax gap can be defined as the amount of money that is earned by people who only report part or non-at-all as taxable income. Also, people who inflate their businesses expenses, so they pay little or no tax, are part of the tax gap problem. The Tax Gap is estimated to be at least $1 trillion to as much as $1.5 trillion.

95% of wage earners who get a *Form W-2* at the end of the year file and pay their taxes. The income is easy to trace, so people have to report it or face the wrath of the IRS.

People who earn money from self-employment, small and large businesses do not file and report their income 50% of the time. Sometimes, they do not report their income at all.

The Biden Administration has proposed that third-party reporters—such as banks and brokerage houses who already have knowledge about the accounts that they have. So, this proposal would require them to report to IRS the inflows and outflows to an existing bank account. It is a simple computer programming change that would vastly improve filing compliance.

The *New York Times* has revealed that while most wage earners pay their fair share of taxes, many business owners engage in blatant fraud at the public's expense. The IRS estimated that Americans report on their taxes less than half of all income that is not subject to some third-party verification, like a *W-2*. Billions of dollars in business profit, rent, and royalties are hidden from the government each year. The tax that would be due on this unreported income is what makes up the Tax Gap.

When you add in all the business that is done in cash and now using credit cards, it is estimated that the Tax Gap is at least $600 billion each year. IRS Director Charles Rettig believes this figure could be a trillion dollars or more.

Cheating has become part of the business fabric of the United States, and it hurts those businesses who are filing and paying their taxes. It also hurts society as a whole because there is not enough

Chapter 17: How Do the *Rich People* Get Away Without Paying Taxes?

money to pay for what "We the People" require in their lives and has made us a debtor nation.

The IRS has become a laughing stock if only every other person is paying taxes, and this makes me mad as hell. As an American Taxpayer, I want a fair and just tax system, and the IRS is the national system set up to deliver the money needed to run the country.

Congress is well aware of the "Tax Gap." Many have personally benefited from the tax gap. Their campaign and reelection funds are flush because of all the money that *Rich People, Big Businesses, and Corporations* have donated to candidates who will not raise their taxes or close tax loopholes.

What the IRS Does to Combat the "Tax Gap"

The IRS used to conduct in-person compliance sweeps. In 1985, I worked on one compliance sweep in Chicago in an eight-block area. We went to every house and business and asked for Social Security or Employer Tax Numbers and then cross-checked them with our IRS computer. About 38% were not filing and paying taxes. The IRS kept this information secret because they felt it might set a precedent for others to cheat if the information was publicized. The IRS used to do reports that would measure the "Tax Gap," but the last time they did that was in 1985.

The IRS knows that some people will try to evade taxes. That is why the IRS is in existence. Fortunately, the current administration is proposing increased funding. There is a bill called the American Families Plan, and it proposes to increase IRS funding by $80 billion to permit the agency to increase audit activity on *Rich People, Big Businesses, and Corporations*.

We cannot allow the IRS to go back to the days where tax collectors used the laws for their own benefits and taxpayers felt abused. (See my earlier book **IRS Whistleblower**, for some of the bad but completely legal things that I did while working for the IRS)

In 2008 Congress passed a bill that required credit card processors to report payments processed online on behalf of retailers using a *Form 1099-K*. I strongly favored that plan, but the Treasury Inspector General in December 2008 reported that the IRS did not have enough personnel or money to investigate the 310,000 cases in which individuals and businesses failed to report more than $433 billion in income documented on *1099-Ks*. After that, the credit card companies sort of made their own rules. The law was watered down so much as to be mostly ineffective.

In 2012, the law was changed to specify that only if a person had more than 200 transactions a year or more than $20,000 in sales would anything be reported to the IRS. So, some people just opened more than one account. Some people use e-Bay and other sites which do not require them to provide their Social Security numbers or Employer Identification Numbers.

Some people starting new businesses do not even try to follow the law and do not register their businesses with the IRS at all. These are ways that the American government loses vital funds to operate our country.

The *Treasury Inspector General for Tax Administration* (TIGTA) reported in 2020 that the IRS had failed to follow up on 369,000 high-income households that simply did not file a tax return in 2016-2018. The *Treasury Inspector General for Tax Administration* reported on March 15, 2020, that between 2014 and 2016, there were nearly 900,000 high-income non-filers, of which 400,000 cases (44% of cases) were never investigated due to resource constraints. Of these 400,000 cases, 300 of the most egregious evaders cost the federal government $10 billion in unpaid taxes over this period.

TIGTA further reported that tax underreporting tends to rise with income when taxpayers are ranked by their total income; this includes the unreported amount. In part, tax evasion rises with higher incomes because higher-income taxpayers have armies of sophisticated tax lawyers, accountants, and tax preparers who can stake out aggressive tax positions that can help shield true tax liability. And because the IRS lacks the number of specialized auditors to detect and pursue this type of non-compliance adequately, the consequences of tax underpayment are perceived to be minor, and voluntary compliance rates are lower.

Tax professionals will always be able to obtain more favorable outcomes for their clients because they know and aggressively prod the IRS into their way of thinking.

Chapter 17: How Do the *Rich People* Get Away Without Paying Taxes?

From 2013 to 2017, the IRS knew that 685,555 taxpayers withheld income over $200,000, thus owing $38.5 billion. However, the IRS did nothing to collect the balances due. The *Treasury Inspector General for Tax Administration* reported March 10, 2021, "High-Income Taxpayers Who Owe Delinquent Taxes Could Be More Effectively Prioritized." It is maddening to many Americans that during this same period of time, middle and low-income taxpayers were prioritized.

High-Income Non-Filers and High-Income Non-Payers are not a priority with the IRS. Thus, some taxpayers take the gamble and stop filing and paying, and they get away with this behavior. More and more people are doing this due to the weakened and depleted state of the IRS.

Big Businesses are Expert at Tax Evasion

All businesses have access to the vast amount of tax write-offs, tax credits, and special rules that they have paid for by actually writing tax laws for Members of Congress. In a **New York Times**, March 10, 2021, Opinion Piece by Chye-Ching Huang, he stated that multinational corporations (*Big Businesses*) being audited by the IRS could outgun and outlast it, stalling their cases as long as possible to run out the statute of limitations.

This is legal but immoral. The tax system only works if all citizens believe that it is fairly enforced.

I believe that making the IRS more transparent about delinquent taxpayers could take care of the details of tax collections from the taxpayers already in the IRS system.

This would free up more money for more resources to pursue those *Rich People, Big Businesses, and Corporations* that do not file or pay at all.

All of the problems of the IRS begin and end with Congress. In the next chapter, I will review the plan outlined by former IRS Commissioners and a Former Secretary of the Treasury who are dedicated to fixing the tax system.

CHAPTER 18

A PROFESSIONAL VIEW FOR THE SOLUTION TO THE TAX GAP

Information on this chapter is from reports written by Fred Goldberg and Charles Rossotti (former IRS Commissioners), Lawrence H. Summers (former Secretary of Treasury), and Natasha Sarin (Law Professor, University of Pennsylvania Law School). Their suggestions are simple to implement and enforce. Details are also available at www.shrinkthetaxgap.com, founded by former IRS Commissioners Charles Rossotti and Fred L. Forman (former IRS Associate Commissioner for Modernization).

Their plan would shrink the tax gap by 19% over ten years, gaining about $1.4 trillion, almost as much as President Biden's current proposal to increase individual income taxes. All of this revenue gain would be from taxpayers in the top 25% income bracket, and most of this would come from increased voluntary compliance. Should the IRS acquire increased efficiency and functionality, it is estimated that for every dollar spent, at least $20 would be collected.

This plan has three elements: (1) fill the gap in information reporting, (2) upgrade computer technology for better processing and tracking, and (3) focus and streamline auditing. This means that the IRS is receiving far more financial tracking information than it can process or use to enforce the tax laws. Their plan also includes reporting income between businesses. This information is easy to collect and audit from banks because it already exists, putting no additional burden on the banks.

They state that the IRS reported that less than half of all income that is not subject to some form of third-party verification like a W-2 is not reported at all. Billions of dollars in business profits, rent, and royalties are hidden from the government each year. Although this is all happening in plain sight and the IRS knows about it, the IRS is unable to do anything to prevent it.

They quote current IRS Commissioner Charles Rettig who said that legally owed unpaid taxes (the tax gap) could "could approach and possibly exceed $1 trillion a year." Rettig also stated that his agency does not have the computer power, employees, or money to do anything about the problem. This is a rare admission by the head of the IRS. It is embarrassing that the IRS has been put into this position by Congress. This is the first time that an IRS official has admitted the fragility of the agency and its near-failure in simply enforcing the law on those unpaid taxes that are due and owing.

The IRS needs $100 billion to be invested in technology and personnel along with a better capability of collecting data on business income over the next ten years to do its job. This would allow the agency to collect $1.4 trillion in lawful tax revenue that would otherwise go uncollected. According to a report prepared by Former IRS Commissioner Charles Rossotti, Harvard economist, Charles Summers and University of Pennsylvania law professor Natasha Sarin argue that since businesses generally report their income about 50% of the time, that all income should be reported on Form 1099 so that it can be tracked and taxed by the IRS. They also argue that the 63-year-old IRS computer system is unable to process, assimilate and use all the financial transactions needed to support the US Tax system. This is crippling the IRS' targets and must be upgraded as soon as possible. I believe it is way past time for this to happen.

People who steal from the system can be called greedy because they are using government services but not paying for them. This is not fair to you, the American taxpayer. We must bring these freeloaders back into the tax-paying fold. Establishing a fair tax system has long been my professional mission.

The actions being proposed to close the tax gap by Rossotti,

Summers, and Sarin do not raise taxes. Their proposal only holds people accountable for the money that they are already receiving and are not reporting. Their suggestions are to make the IRS enforce the laws that are already on the books.

Former Treasury Secretary, Lawrence Summers said, "My most important recommendation in the tax area would be that we could collect $1 trillion over the next decade, at least from better enforcement on the $7 trillion that is owed, but not paid, with most of that coming from the richest taxpayers." As it stands now, he noted, "Many high-income earners (income over $100,000) are not filing taxes and getting away with it." A report by the *Treasury Inspector General for Tax Administration* (TIGTA) has identified nearly 880,000 *High-Income Non-Filers*, with an estimated taxes due of $45.7 billion.

Former IRS Commissioners Charles Rossetti and Fred Goldberg have both advocated plans that will help the IRS recover and become vital and functional again. I worked under both of these gentlemen, and they were the most progressive, hands-on, problem-solving commissioners I have ever seen.

My experience is that generally, wage earners try to do the right thing in their financial and tax affairs. However, taxpayers need to be aware that the IRS may look at their tax records and come up with different conclusions than they had in their tax returns. (Please see Chapter 7).

The 63-year-old IRS computer system is currently linked together in a massive ancient cobweb utilizing the language Fortran, Basic, and Cobalt. The need for the IRS to have better computer technology is obvious and needs to be addressed by Congress.

The evident benefit of increased funding to the IRS for better technology is the effect it will have on all the taxpayers who are trying to file, pay, and respond to collection and audit notices. The whole system is dysfunctional when only 29% of the 100 million telephone calls received in 2019 were answered. Additionally, it routinely takes four to six months to get a response from the IRS. If you write to them.

EPILOGUE

RECOMMENDATIONS FOR IRS AND CONGRESS 2021–2022

Nobody likes to pay taxes, but most people recognize that any functioning nation or society needs to have taxes to support its common goals. These taxes should only be taken from people's surplus wealth. Each citizen is entitled to a reasonable standard of living. The Talmud says that people who do not pay or evade taxes should be regarded as a common thief—robbing the public.

Taxes need to be fair and just. Taxes in the United States favor *Rich People, Big Businesses, and Corporations* and do not provide for all the people's good and welfare. Irresponsible spending has forced an enormous burden on our country and the children of the future. The United States owes $28.4 trillion to investors who loaned it money. No one talks about this! Technically, the United States is insolvent and bankrupt at this moment. We need both a national wake-up call and need to see how this happened and who got all the money.

The Government tells you to pay taxes; the Bible tells you to pay taxes; Jesus paid his taxes; your boss takes your taxes out of your paycheck before you receive it. The result of your paying federal, state, and local taxes is witnessed by you every day. The military, social benefit programs, Social Security, Medicare, roads, bridges, and education protect all of us. These are essential in providing for the well-being and continuation of our society.

Congress is not working for "We the People." It is very much working for the *Rich People, Big Businesses, and Corporations*. We must stop the influence-peddling on the members of Congress. No dirty "backroom deals" should be tolerated.

It does not matter if you like to pay taxes or not. Taxes are here to stay. Working with the system to make taxes reasonable for the people who are expected to pay them is the challenge, and Congress can make those positive changes. **However, Congress has cut the IRS budget for most of the last 12 years. This does not help our society.** For every $1 that is cut out from the IRS budget, $6 goes uncollected.

We have to do something quickly to revive the IRS. At this point in time, the IRS and American public are losing. One could say there are five main reasons for this crisis:

- 52,000 out of 62,000 full time IRS employees are slated to retire in the next six years. This leads to hiring new agents. Training new agents and officers with the subsequent gap between experience and inexperienced employees will be a serious issue. The IRS is currently advertising to hire 682 new *Revenue Officers*, but with their internal training structure, that would mean that 239 existing *Revenue Officers* would need to be deployed for at least one-year full time to be classroom instructors and on the job coaches. The IRS is also hiring 1300 *Revenue Agents* and 500 *Criminal Special Agents* in the Fall 2021.
- The IRS is dealing with a 63-year-old computer system that utilizes outdated languages such as Fortran or Cobalt.
- Social Security suffers when people don't pay the taxes due to the system. This destroys the future benefits for the workers while depleting the Social Security "banks."

- With the Covid-19 pandemic, many Americans have faced long-term unemployment, medical bills, housing issues to name a few. The payment of taxes on unemployment benefits coupled with changing addresses due to eviction or loss of jobs reveals a potential loss of tax revenue.
- The new tax rules from 2017 have changed the public's focus on paying taxes. If the wealthy pay only $1.00 in taxes, then why should the regular American pay any taxes?

Just a quick reminder, this is one of the reasons that I wrote this book. I witnessed the IRS routinely harassing people who owe under $100,000 with letters, bank, and wage levies, while *Rich People, Big Businesses, and Corporations* are left alone. What I see is tens of millions of self-employed people avoid and underreport their taxes, millions more who do not file or pay any taxes at all. Even though the IRS knows about this situation, the agency is limited in its ability to collect from those people, so it picks on the lower-income wage earner. To me, it is just not fair!

Small Changes Bring Great Rewards

The most basic changes will bring great rewards. Since seventy-five percent of business is now conducted electronically, it leaves a trail that the IRS can easily follow. That is the basis for the recommendations made in the report provided by Former IRS Commissioner Charles Rossotti.

Congress could enforce the tax law for the millions who do not pay anything at all now. These are self-employed people, *Rich People, Big Businesses, and Corporations*. The IRS could also make immediate changes in their operating procedures and attitude that will make what they are supposed to do, i.e., do audits and collect unpaid taxes fairer and more efficient.

Congress Needs to Make Laws That Will:

1. Add a wealth tax on the top 2% if they make or have more than $50 million and 3% if they make

more than $1 billion in wages, gains, asset sales, interest, dividends, or related income and asset increases.

2. Eliminate Income Taxes for individuals who make $40,000 or $80,000 per couple. They still would pay Social Security and Medicare taxes. They would also have a direct option to purchase Government Bonds to secure their futures.

3. Expand the estate tax. Only 0.02% of estates pay any tax.

4. Institute a Value Added Tax (VAT), a tax on goods manufactured and later sold indirectly by the consumer.

5. Give the Social Security Administration and the Department of Health and Human Services the legal authority to administer the Earned Income Tax Credit Program, Child Tax Credits, Credit for Other Dependents, Child and Dependent Tax Credit, Adoption Tax Credit, American Opportunity Credit, Lifetime Learning Credit, Student Loan Interest Tax Credit. These are all social service programs that Congress uses to encourage certain types of activities. The IRS has no business administering social service programs.

6. Eliminate the married filing status, head of the household status, and married filing separately status.

7. Eliminate stepped-up basis.

8. Eliminate carried-interest loophole.

9. Cap-like-kind exchanges.

10. Eliminate payroll tax loophole.

11. Make the IRS follow the laws Congress enacted regarding *Offers in Compromise*. Make this a viable option in every case. This would generate billions of dollars.

12. Institute a National Income Tax Filing Lottery. Americans love to think that they are going to get something for nothing. Prizes awarded would be taxable. That would build up future filing compliance and probably attract millions of people who do not even file tax returns right now. We should have a national lottery tied in with the income tax system, which would cause many people to file to have a chance at winning the prizes.

13. Allow the IRS to apply the balance of the *IRS Excess Collections File* to the general I.R.S budget appropriation. The *Excess Collections* consists of all monies received by the IRS that they cannot identify who send them or where they are to be applied to. In 2016 TIGTA reported that this *secret account* had a balance in it of $5.8 billion. It has probably increased by another $5 billion since that time. Open government should not have secret bank accounts.

14. The IRS has other secret accounts. These include the "Unclaimed Refund account, which usually has $1.5 billion-plus in it.

15. The IRS has access to another $5-7 billion in tax monies that were collected from illegal immigrants working regular jobs. They will never have access to that money. My question is, who is monitoring these accounts, and where the money disappears to?

A flat tax is never the solution to this because it is a regressive tax. That means that the impact of paying the tax falls harder on the poor than on the rich. This has attracted many people, but it is not a viable option. A regressive tax system may seem to appear an equitable form of taxation, regardless of income level, where everyone pays the same amount of tax. In reality, such a tax causes lower-income groups to pay a greater proportion of their income than higher-income groups pay. Regressive taxes are used in the following circumstances:

- A flat tax
- Gasoline tax, tobacco or alcohol taxes, taxes on jewelry, perfume, or travel
- User fees, like business or professional licenses,
- Fees for hunting or fishing licenses
- Tolls for roads or bridges
- Fees for parking
- Fees for entry to museums, parks, and monuments.

What the IRS Can Do Right Now to Refocus on their Mission

Goals:

The philosophy of the Internal Revenue Service should change to finding out what they can collect or assess through an audit, right here, right now, in making case selection determinations. This includes the automatic use of installment agreements and *Currently Not Collectible* determinations, and also the use of *Offers in Compromise*. This precludes the need for a tax amnesty.

- Each Social Security number should be assigned a PIN to prevent identity fraud. In the future, a system should be implemented where a taxpayer uses a thumbprint to sign their tax documents or facial recognition.

- Make cost-effective plans to maximize taxes collected.

- Get a new computer system—their current system is 63 years old.

- The IRS should stop trying to draw a line in the sand and prove a point with people who refuse to pay their taxes due to moral, constitutional, anti-war, or other reasons to protest. So much money is being spent there that could be going to other places where their efforts would result in increased filing and paying compliance.

- IRS employees should be encouraged to be reasonable and use their judgment to "do the right thing" and care about the taxpayers whose cases they are assigned to work on and make sound financial judgments and tax evaluations based on the financial circumstances of each taxpayer.

- Reasonable deadlines and expectations should be stressed in all communications with taxpayers. Right now, the IRS tells you to hurry up and give them money or information, and then you spend months or years waiting for a response.

- If the IRS had a website where taxpayers could report changes in their circumstances, this would save a lot of time in collection and audit and even criminal cases later. If a person had gone through unemployment or other financial loss or has filed bankruptcy, this would be reported. If they suffered any financial hardship or mental/physical breakdowns, these could all be reported. An indicator on the system would classify them and decide if that could affect the case status in the future.

- IRS should post on each taxpayer's account their current status of every case. For example, if a case is inactive, collection status with a Revenue Officer or taxpayer is *Currently Not Collectible Due to Financial Hardship*.

- IRS should post the *Collection Statute Expiration Date* (CSED) on each taxpayer's account. IRS should also explain when that date occurs that the taxpayer will no longer owe the outstanding tax balances.

- The IRS needs to be able to serve taxpayers 24/7. An interactive website and the use of email would allow this to happen.

- Each IRS employee should provide their eFax phone number and their email address to reduce the burden taxpayers have in reaching IRS employees working on their cases.

- Focus all collection efforts on those in the top 20% of income earners (over $100,000) for non-filed returns and balances due.

- The circumstances of every *Offer in Compromise* that is accepted should be published with their name, age, address, amount due, and amount settled for. Additionally, the offer being accepted was in the best interests of the Government.

- All cases where penalties are being assessed should automatically be reviewed for the case history to determine if they meet the *First-Time Penalty Abatement Waiver* automatically without the taxpayer having to apply for it. That said, the taxpayer should be informed in a letter why the penalty was not applied. I propose a freeze on all tax penalties for three years due to Covid-19 and allow US citizens to catch up. The IRS should not be collecting penalties and interest from people who are suffering from Covid-19 and life.

- All taxpayers should have immediate access to their current and past three years' tax records online. This was put into the law and has never occurred. The present system does not let up to 40% of taxpayers pass the requirements to do this.

Audit

- Audits should be the goal in the same or following year, not three years after the tax return is filed.

- Each case should be coded with its DIF score, and the IRS should publish this.

- Focus audit efforts on the top 20% of income earners (business and personal taxpayers).

- If audit yield is expected to be less than $10,000, the IRS should bypass the case. Suppose the IRS has information that indicates that any proposed adjustment will not be collectible. In that case, it should not propose any tax increase. I advocate taxpayer education over taxpayer punishment.

- The IRS also needs to look at what they audited in the past. They need to determine why the IRS has such a high percentage of audits that have resulted in increased refunds or those audits that have resulted in no change in the tax due. It is ridiculous to continue to use outdated and outmoded audit selection methods.

- IRS audits of large corporations have a no-change rate of almost 55%. Audits that consume IRS resources for sometimes years at time can inefficiently consume IRS resources and burden taxpayers who are compliant with the tax laws. The IRS needs to select the most productive audit targets that will result in new tax assessments.

- Audit cases should be reviewed for collectability—if there is not going to be a chance of ever collecting the money that will be assessed, then the case should be closed.

- Taxpayer education should be emphasized over financially penalizing the taxpayer. All business taxpayers should be required to watch an IRS video outlining their duties and responsibilities as a business owner and an employer. They should be required to watch a follow-up video every year as part of their continuing business education certification. This will help many business owners deal with the IRS and make tough business decisions regarding letting employees go or restructuring their business to make them more profitable. Profitable businesses in tax compliance are good for the Government and the people of the United States.

- Computer matching should be done on all documents required to be filed before tax refunds over $10,000 are issued. This is not possible now because the law does not require the 1099 and K-1 forms to be filed before the returns are due. A human being should do reviews. Suspicious cases will be referred higher up the line.

- IRS should skip one year of audits to make it more current with tax audits. Since the tax laws changed drastically in 2017, skipping 2018 audits would not be without precedent as no income taxes were collected in 1943. That was the year when the W-2 wage collection was introduced.

- A council should be convened, lasting for one year of Enrolled Agents, CPAs, and Tax Attorneys, actually working in the field to review and suggest changes that would streamline the IRS audit and collection systems and make it fairer. It should be matched with employees from all IRS departments who are actual employees, not management officials.

The *New York Times* estimated that $1 trillion more could be collected if the IRS was adequately funded, had new technology, and hired more employees. Ex-Commissioner Charles Rossotti suggests as much as $1.6 trillion more could be collected. (See Chapter 17).

IRS management shares in the responsibility for the direction of the IRS. When *ProPublica*'s report came out showing how little America's wealthiest people pay in taxes, IRS Commissioner Charles Rettig announced he would try to prosecute the leaker. Rettig was appointed by President Trump. From an article in the **DAILY BEAST** by Sion Bell and Jeff Hauser, they state that prior to this appointment, Rettig worked at a law firm in Beverly Hills specializing in shielding wealthy taxpayers from IRS audits. "In 2010, when the IRS announced the creation of a task force focused on auditing the very wealthy, Rettig publicly denounced the task force's work as 'Audits from hell,' a particularly troubling pronouncement from someone now in charge of said audits".

Sion Bell and Jeff Hauser go on to state, "President Biden should see Rettig for who he is: a Trump appointee installed to protect the interests of the wealthy, including but not limited to Trump himself, above all else. By immediately fore fronting the tenuous and suspect privacy concerns of billionaires, Rettig's response to the ProPublica reporting is just the latest display of his fundamental allegiance. If Biden is truly committed to reforming our tax system by finally making the wealthy pay their fair share, he will exercise his clear legal authority and replace Rettig at the helm of the IRS"

My purpose in writing this book is to provide taxpayers who owe the IRS the opportunity to learn secrets to obtain fair *installment agreement* terms or have their cases declared *currently not collectible* due to financial hardship. I believe that secrets do not belong in tax administration. My personal goals are:

- I don't want the *Rich People, Big Businesses* or *Corporations* to pay for everything. I want them to pay their fair share.
- I don't want to dissolve Congress; I want the Congress to represent "We the People" and not special interests parties who give them big bucks to influence and control them.
- I don't want *Big Businesses* and *Corporations* to be unprofitable; but I want them out of the tax regulatory and policy making processes.

The Tax System in the United States of America needs to change. There is no better time for that to start happening then right now.

IRS ABBREVIATIONS

ACS	Automated Collection System
ALE	Allowable Living Expenses
AMT	Alternative Minimum Tax
AUR	Automatic Under-Reporter System
CAP	Collection Appeals Program
CDPA	Collection Due Process Appeal
CFS	Collection Financial Statement
CI	Criminal Investigations
CIS	Collection Information Statement
CSED	Collection Statue of Expiration Date
DDIA	Direct Debt Installment Agreement
EFTPS	Electronic Funds Tax Payment System
EIDL	Economic Injury Disaster Loans
EITC	Earned Income Tax Credit
FPLP	Federal Payment Levy Program
FTAN	First Time Penalty Abatement Waiver
GHW	Global High Wealth
IA	Installment Agreement
IAC	Interest Abatement Coordinator
IAUF	Installment Agreement User Fees
IRC	Internal Revenue Code
IRM	Internal Revenue Manual
LITCs	Low Income Taxpayer Clinics
NFTL	Notice of Federal Tax Lien
OIC	Offer in Compromise
RA	Revenue Agent

R/O	Field Revenue Officer
SFR	Substitution for Returns
TCE	Tax Counseling for the Elderly
TCO	Tax Compliance Officer
TEs	Tax Examiners
TFRP	Trust Fund Recovery Penalty
VITA	Volunteer Income Tax Assistance

IF YOU NEED HELP

If you cannot find a tax resolution professional, I will help you. As an Enrolled Agent, I am nationally licensed by the IRS to help people with tax issues. You can call me for a free confidential 15-minute consultation at 520-448-3531. My prices are fair and reasonable, and you are getting 40 years of tax knowledge and experience to help you in your situation.

RMS Tax Consulting LLC
Richard M. Schickel
Enrolled Agent
520-448-3531
richard@rmstaxconsulting.com
http://rmstaxconsulting.com/

ACKNOWLEDGMENTS

Eternally grateful for the brilliant editing skills of Katherine Thompson of Paris & Cosmo LLC, Tucson, AZ.

Thanks to Mario Castañeda for cover design and graphic arts.

Thanks to Melissa Williams Design for interior formatting and editing.

Also by Richard M. Schickel

What to Do When the IRS is After You: Secrets of the IRS as Revealed by Retired IRS Employees

IRS Whistleblower

Why the IRS Doesn't Work Anymore

Gifts of the Spirit: My Mission as a Healer

ABOUT THE AUTHOR

RICHARD M. SCHICKEL was a Senior Revenue Officer (Tax Collector) with the Internal Revenue Service for 33 years. He was awarded the Medal of Meritorious Service by Donald Regan, Secretary of the Treasury. He received sixty-six awards from the IRS. He is considered to be a subject matter expert for the IRS Collection System.

Upon his retirement he became an Enrolled Agent licensed to practice before the Internal Revenue Service nationally. He founded RMS Tax Consulting LLC in Tucson, Arizona and Chicago, Illinois with a group of retired IRS. Agents, so that he could continue to serve people in trouble with the IRS.

He has published tax articles in the *Journal of Tax Practice and Procedure* by Wolters Kluwer, the *Arizona Republic*, and the *Arizona Daily Star*. He co-authored the Internal Revenue Manual §5.15 "Financial Analysis" and has authored four books: *IRS Whistleblower, What to Do When the IRS is After You, The Asset Recovery Guide,* and *Inside the IRS* set to be released in October, 2021.

SOURCES

"Shrinking the Tax Gap: Approaches and Revenue Potential" Natasha Sarin and Lawrence H. Summers, November 2019
https://www.nber.org/system/files/working_papers/w26475/w26475.pdf

Rossotti, Summers and Sarin
Shrinking the Tax Gap: A Comprehensive Approach
https://shrinkthetaxgap.com/shrinking-the-tax-gap-november-30-2020/

"Make Tax System Fairer, Easier for Taxpayers While Collecting $1.4 Trillion Owed but Not Paid" Fred Goldberg and Charles Rossotti, February 17, 2021

Tax Reform for Progressivity: A Pragmatic Approach. Sarin, Summers and Kupferberg.
https://www.brookings.edu/wp-content/uploads/2020/01/SarinSummers_LO_FINAL.pdf

Understanding the Revenue Potential of Tax Compliance Investment
Sarin and Summers
September 8, 2020
https://www.nber.org/papers/w27571

Shrink the Tax Gap
Forman, Goldberg and Rossotti
https://shrinkthetaxgap.com/shrink-the-tax-gap-presentation/

Lawrence H. Summers and Natasha Sarin: If business leaders are serious about doing good, they can start by paying their taxes
https://www.washingtonpost.com/opinions/2020/01/30/if-business-leaders-are-serious-about-doing-good-they-can-start-by-paying-their-taxes/

Lawrence H. Summers and Natasha Sarin: Yes, our tax system needs reform. Let's start with this first step.
https://www.washingtonpost.com/opinions/yes-our-tax-system-needs-reform-lets-start-with-this-first-step/2019/11/17/4d23f8d4-07dd-11ea-924a-28d87132c7ec_story.html

The Post's View: The IRS cannot keeping trying to do more with less https://www.washingtonpost.com/opinions/the-irs-cannot-keep-trying-to-do-more-with-less/2019/05/28/1b3122d4-7caa-11e9-8bb7-0fc796cf2ec0_story.html

Five Former IRS Commissioners Agree
05-05-2021
https://www.washingtonpost.com/opinions/five-former-irs-commissioners-bidens-proposal-would-create-a-fairer-tax-system/2021/05/04/c4ee8346-acfc-11eb-ab4c-986555a1c511_story.html

Rossotti Testifies Before the Senate Finance Committee
https://www.finance.senate.gov/imo/media/doc/SFC%20written%20submission%20final05082021.pdf

https://www.americanprogress.org/issues/economy/reports/2021/04/19/498311/better-tax-enforcement-can-advance-fairness-raise-1-trillion-revenue/

Study on Tax Evasion by Reck, Risch, and Zucman.
https://www.nber.org/papers/w28542

Make the Tax System Fairer.
https://news.bloomberglaw.com/daily-tax-report/make-tax-system-fairer-easier-for-taxpayers-while-collecting-1-4-trillion-owed-but-not-paid

www.ingramcontent.com/pod-product-compliance
Lightning Source LLC
Chambersburg PA
CBHW070623220526
45466CB00001B/82